VEGETARIAN DINNER in MINUTES

75 RECIPES FOR QUICK AND EASY EVERYDAY MEALS

By Linda Gassenheimer   *Photographs by Jennifer Lévy*

CHRONICLE BOOKS

SAN FRANCISCO

Library of Congress Cataloging-in-Publication Data:

Gassenheimer, Linda.
    Vegetarian dinner in minutes: 75 recipes for quick and easy everyday meals/by Linda Gassenheimer.
        p. cm.
    Includes index.
    ISBN 0-8118-1383-5 (pb)
    1. Vegetarian cookery. 2. Cookery, International. 3. Quick and easy cookery. I.   Title.
    TX837.G323 1997
    641.5'636-dc21   96-51121
                                                          CIP

Printed in Hong Kong.

Designed by Deb Miner, designer

Distributed in Canada by Raincoast Books
8680 Cambie Street
Vancouver, British Columbia V6P 6M9

10 9 8 7 6 5 4 3 2 1

Chronicle Books
85 Second Street
San Francisco, California 94105

Web Site: www.chronbooks.com

To my family—Harold, James, John, and Charles—
and my sister and brother-in-law, Roberta and Robert,
for their advice, enthusiasm, and patience.

ACKNOWLEDGMENTS

As I sit at my computer I realize that writing can be a lonely task. It's my readers, editors, friends, and family that make this an exciting two-way street. I thank them all for their enthusiastic support.

My biggest thanks go to my husband, Harold, who not only tested the food and washed the dishes, but helped edit every word.

Sitting down to a table of several dinners waiting to be taste-tested is fun once in a while, but on a weekly basis it can be a difficult duty. My son James did it with a smile. And my sons Charles and John never complained about missing their favorite dishes when they came to visit. I want to thank them for being my best supporters.

My "Dinner in Minutes" column in the *Miami Herald* just celebrated its ninth anniversary. I'd like to thank current and past supporters for their help: features editor Elissa Vanover, former food editor Felicia Gressette, current food editor Kathy Martin, and Fred Tasker, writer of the wine suggestions for my column.

I delight in my enduring relationship with Judith Weber, my literary agent, who continues to guide me with enthusiasm to exciting projects.

Working with an editor three thousand miles away can be difficult. But my editor, Bill LeBlond, has melted the miles away and is both a delightful friend and a wonderful editor.

Gardner's Markets is not only a family-owned and family-run chain of four fine-food supermarkets, it's a family in itself. I'd like to thank all of my colleagues there for their friendship and interest. Most of all, I'd like to thank Elizabeth Gardner Adams and her husband, Maurice, for the opportunity to help create an exciting food and wine environment.

Most important, I'd like to thank everyone who reads this book and prepares these dinners. I hope you will enjoy the recipes as much as I have enjoyed creating them.

CONTENTS

FOREWORD

I've had a love affair with beautiful produce for years. It began when I lived in Paris and shopped at the open street markets. In a style typical of the French, the market stalls were each set with precision and care. There were abundant displays of green, red, and yellow peppers, shiny red tomatoes, and bunches of freshly picked herbs that enticed me to take them home. While shooting photographs in London for my first cookbook, I became so enthralled by the colors, textures, and aromas of the wild mushrooms that they were featured on the cover of the book.

When I travel, one of my favorite activities is to ask chefs I meet to take me on a tour of the street markets to view the local produce. Their eyes always light up—they can't wait to tell me about their local culture and share their great recipes with me. My Jamaican Okra Stew was created after such a tour. The Sweet and Sour Mushrooms recipe came from a similar visit to Hong Kong's famous street markets.

I had an opportunity to replicate the exciting atmosphere of street produce markets working with the farmers in South Florida and creating a farmers' market outside of Gardner's Markets. The farmers trucked in their freshest produce and staffed the booths. I was thrilled with the community's support for the farmers and its interest in trying new products.

This book documents my love of the fruit of the earth and the inspiration it gives me to cook.

INTRODUCTION

When I created a farmers' market in Miami, I was surprised by some of the questions I received from vendors and customers alike. "How do I get more vegetables into my life?" "How do I cook this?" "What does it go with?" "How can I get my kids to eat more vegetables?" "How can I make my vegetables taste good?" These questions, coupled with requests from my readers for more vegetarian dinners, prompted me to start writing some vegetarian meals for my syndicated Miami Herald *column, "Dinner in Minutes." ¶ As I began to develop new recipes, I realized that most vegetarian dishes take a lot of time to prepare, with lots of chopping and peeling, and usually get their flavor from the use of a lot of fat. ¶ When I get home from work, I need quick, delicious, and healthful dinners for my family. This book meets these demands with simplified buying and cooking techniques. The recipes call for one-stop supermarket shopping, require as little chopping and measuring as possible, and provide varied, healthy dinners with 30 percent or less of the calories coming from fat.*

QUICK SHOPPING All the ingredients for these recipes can be bought at your local supermarket. One-stop shopping is as important as quick cooking. Each dinner has its own shopping list showing the amounts you need. I have supplied container, can, and package sizes to make it easy. If in your area the sizes are different, buy the amount needed in the most efficient size. The staples list provided with each recipe helps you organize your pantry. If you

[**PICTURED**: *Vegetable Curry with Toasted Rice Pilaf, page 114*]

have these ingredients on hand, you will need to pick up only a few fresh ingredients to complete the recipe.

QUICK COOKING TECHNIQUES Vegetarian cooking generally requires a lot of ingredient preparation. I tackle this problem by taking advantage of what the supermarket has to offer—packaged washed salads, peeled baby carrots, precut stir-fry vegetables—items that help cut down on preparation time. Using the food processor for chopping and slicing is another time-saver.

My recipes are also designed to reduce preparation time. Measuring by cups and spoonfuls is time consuming. If you are slicing celery in the food processor, you may wonder how many stalks you need to make one cup. To make it easy, I call for two celery stalks. You don't have to measure the celery. If you come out with a half-cup more or less, it won't affect the recipe. Until you feel secure with this type of measuring, you can use the exact measurements, which are also provided, as a guide.

My recipes call for ingredients such as a medium tomato, potato, or cucumber. For the most part, these are standard sizes throughout the country. If you are concerned about the definition of sizes, buy what you think is medium-sized and measure it against the cup measurements in the recipe. You will then have your own measuring guide and you won't have to bother measuring the next time.

The **COUNTDOWN** section of the recipes organizes your cooking schedule with an outline of the steps for preparing the dinners. To me, there's nothing more frustrating than popping a dish in the oven and realizing that I haven't preheated it, or having to slow down a meal because I forgot to put the pasta water on to boil.

In the **HELPFUL HINTS** section of the recipes I share cooking tips with you. The cooking techniques I learned while training with several chefs and for my Cordon Bleu degree have been a great help in developing these dinners. Knowing where I can take shortcuts and where I can't helps me create dinners that are quick but still tasty. The simple hints can be transferred to other recipes and will become part of your own cooking habits.

HEALTHY EATING *Vegetarian Dinner in Minutes* is a cooking lifestyle. All of the dinners are within the government guidelines for fat intake of 30 percent of total calories consumed. You can eat your way through this book without worrying about the fat content of individual dishes. A particular salad dressing may have a high percentage of fat, but when balanced with the other dishes in the meal, the ratio of fat to calories is correct.

Using less fat means you need to get as much flavor as possible from the ingredients. Use top-quality olive oil and fresh Parmesan cheese. You are buying less, so buy the best.

EXCITING INTERNATIONAL FLAVORS This book is organized into flavors from around the world. During my twenty years in Europe, I discovered that the cuisines of the Mediterranean—from Provence to the Middle East—use herbs, nuts, and grains to create simple food with complex flavors. These flavors are captured in Wild Mushroom Risotto and Creamed Spinach, Roasted Red Pepper Pasta with Sautéed Escarole and Chickpeas, and Tabbouleh with Toasted Walnut Couscous.

Intriguing Chinese and Indian foods have always been favorites of mine. While on trips to the Far East, I learned more about their use of herbs and flavors. I tasted wonderful combinations that inspired Black Pepper "Tenderloin" with Sesame Noodles and Chinese Steamboat.

The hot, earthy flavors of Tex-Mex and the Southwest formed the basis for another chapter. Pan-Grilled

Quesadillas have become a favorite of mine both for dinner and for hors d'oeuvres. I had some left over one night and froze them. When friends stopped by unexpectedly, I whisked them out for a perfect snack with drinks. Chiles en Nogada (Stuffed Chiles in Walnut Sauce) with Pimiento Rice is another star in my household.

When I first came to Miami in 1986, I was fascinated with the hot, spicy flavors of the Caribbean. Try the Cuban-influenced Arroz con Garbanzo (Spanish Rice and Beans) with Tossed Greens. Through visits to New Orleans, I became acquainted with hot Cajun. For a quick Cajun meal, the Cajun Kabobs with Creole Rice and Red Beans is perfect.

And finally, American comfort foods are back in style, but with a new twist. Grilled Portobello Steak Sandwich with Garlic French Fries and All-American Pepper, Mushroom and Onion Pizza with Panzanella Salad (Bread Salad) are two delicious variations on old favorites.

I tested these dinners on family, friends and many who scoff at vegetarian meals, thinking they are bland and uninteresting. They passed their scrutiny. I hope you enjoy making these dinners—in minutes.

QUICK COOKING TIPS *Knowing your way around the kitchen will help you get your meal on the table in minutes. Here are some tips to help you along.*

➤ When preparing a recipe for the first time, read it all the way through, and then prepare the ingredients. Place the ingredients on cutting boards or in bowls easily accessible to your work area.

➤ The spices in these recipes can be found in the spice section of the supermarket. Spices lose their flavor and strength if kept longer than six months, so be sure to replenish your supply as needed.

➤ Buy good-quality Parmesan cheese. Ask the grocer to grate it for you or grate it at home in the food processor. Freeze extra cheese in a sealable plastic container for later use. You can spoon out what you need and leave the rest frozen.

➤ Red onion is used in many of these recipes. It's a sweet onion, available year-round. If other sweet onions, such as Vidalia or Texas Sweet, are available in your area, use them instead.

➤ Olive oil spray is available in most supermarkets. If you prefer to use bottled olive oil, pour some into a clean spray bottle. Each spray deposits about ¼ teaspoon of oil.

➤ When you buy vegetable broth in 14½-ounce cans and need 2 cups, use water to fill the second cup rather than opening a new can.

➤ To save time peeling carrots, use peeled baby carrots. About 20 sliced baby carrots equal 1 cup.

➤ To wash parsley, watercress, or other fresh herbs quickly, immerse the leaves in a bowl of water for several minutes. When you lift the herb out of the bowl, sand and dirt will be left behind.

➤ To chop fresh herbs quickly and cleanly, cut sprigs with a scissors over a bowl or glass.

➤ To peel garlic quickly, firmly press each clove with the side of a knife. The papery skin will easily fall off or peel away. Or, buy peeled garlic cloves, which will last at least one week in the refrigerator.

➤ To crush garlic quickly, use a good-quality garlic press. The press can also be used to crush peeled fresh ginger.

➤ To use the food processor most efficiently, first chop all the dry ingredients, such as walnuts, and then the wet ingredients, such as onions. This way, you don't have to stop in the middle of cooking to wash the processor bowl.

➤ To make marinating easy and also save washing a bowl, use a resealable plastic bag instead of a bowl or pan. To turn vegetables, simply flip the bag over.

➤ To avoid using an extra bowl when making salad dressing, mix it in the bottom of the salad bowl, then add the salad and toss.

➤ Use several small chopping boards when cooking. They can be carried to the stove and you won't have to stop and wash boards while working.

➤ When bringing water to a boil, cover the pot to speed the process.

➤ For quick cooking, a large pot or frying pan is best as it brings more food into direct contact with the heat.

➤ To boil or sauté potatoes quickly, cut them into small chunks. Potatoes should be washed but don't need to be peeled before using.

➤ To make ten-minute rice, cook it like pasta. Place it in a large pot of boiling water for 10 minutes, then drain in a colander and dress it with sauce, oil, or butter.

➤ To speed up stir-frying, place all of the prepared ingredients on a plate or cutting board in order of use. This way, you won't have to keep looking at the recipe to see which ingredient to add next.

➤ For best stir-frying results, make sure your wok or frying pan is very hot before you start to stir-fry.

➤ To get a quick high- or low-heat response from electric burners, keep two burners heated, one on high, one on low, and move your pot back and forth between them.

STAPLES

Quick shopping is as important as fast cooking. I find that stocking my shelves with certain staples means that I need to run into the supermarket for only a few ingredients. Here is a staples list to help you organize your kitchen.

CHILLED PRODUCE

Carrots

Celery

Fresh orange juice

Garlic

Lemon

Red onion

Yellow onion

CONDIMENTS

Capers

Dijon mustard

Honey

Horseradish

Hot pepper sauce

Low-salt soy sauce

Mayonnaise (low fat)

Salad dressing (low fat
  or fat-free)

Worcestershire sauce

DAIRY

Butter or margarine

Eggs

Nonfat plain yogurt

Parmesan cheese
  (grated and frozen
  or freshly grated)

Skim milk

CANNED INGREDIENTS

Black beans

Cannellini or
  white navy beans

Chickpeas

Crushed tomatoes

Low-salt tomato sauce

Red kidney beans

Tomato paste

Tomato purée

Vegetable broth

Whole tomatoes

DRY GOODS

All-purpose unbleached
  white flour
Arborio or Valencia rice
Cornstarch
Dried linguine or fettuccine
Egg noodles
Lentils
Long-grain white rice
Orzo
Plain bread crumbs
Precooked couscous
Quick-cooking brown rice
Raisins
Salt
Sugar
White basmati rice

OILS

Canola oil
Olive oil
Olive oil spray
Sesame oil

VINEGARS

Balsamic vinegar
Distilled white vinegar
Oriental rice wine vinegar
Red wine vinegar

WINES

Dry sherry
Dry vermouth
Dry white wine

SPICES

Black peppercorns
Cayenne pepper
Chili powder
Curry powder
Dark brown sugar
Dried oregano
Dried rosemary
Dried sage
Dried thyme
Ground allspice
Ground cardamom
Ground cinnamon
Ground coriander
Ground cumin
Ground nutmeg
Paprika

GLOSSARY

ALLSPICE: A berry from the pimiento tree found in West Indian and South American countries that tastes like a combination of nutmeg, cloves, and cinnamon.

ARBORIO RICE: A short-grain Italian rice that is used to make risotto. Its high starch content produces a creamy texture.

BASMATI RICE: An aromatic long-grain rice from India and Pakistan that smells something like popcorn when it cooks. An American version is grown in the United States.

BIJOL: A yellow-colored spice used in many Latin dishes, bijol may be substituted for saffron or turmeric. It is made from ground annatto seed, and often contains some cumin and oregano.

BULGUR WHEAT: Wheat kernels that have been steamed, dried, and crushed.

CARDAMOM: An East Indian spice with a sweet, slightly spicy flavor. It can be bought as a seed in a pod or ground.

CHAKCHOUKA: A cooked tomato salad from North Africa.

CHAYOTE (CHRISTOPHENE): A member of the gourd family, chayote resembles a green, gnarled pear. It can be grated, boiled, or stuffed, and can be eaten raw or cooked.

CHIPOTLE CHILE PEPPER: A smoked jalapeño pepper, sold dried, canned, or pickled.

CORIANDER: An herb with tan-colored seeds that are used mostly for pickling. Ground coriander is commonly used as a spice in sweet and savory dishes. The green coriander leaves, also known as cilantro and Chinese parsley, are widely used in Latin and Asian dishes.

COUSCOUS: A pasta made by moistening semolina and rolling it in flour to form tiny balls. Precooked couscous, the type most commonly found in supermarkets, takes only five minutes to cook.

ESCAROLE: A large, flat, slightly curly pale green leaf lettuce. Escarole has a mild flavor in salads and can also be used as a cooked vegetable.

FENNEL: A pale green bulb, sometimes called anise, with feathery leaves similar to dill. Fennel has a slightly sweet licorice flavor when raw and a pleasant, very mild flavor when cooked.

FETA CHEESE: A traditional Greek cheese made from goat's or sheep's milk. Commercial feta is often made from cow's milk.

FILÉ POWDER: A spice made from dried sassafras leaves, used to thicken and flavor gumbos and other Creole dishes. It can be found in the spice section of the supermarket.

FUSILLI PASTA: A thick, corkscrew-shaped spaghetti that is usually about 2 inches long.

GORGONZOLA CHEESE: An Italian, soft, mild blue cheese.

JICAMA: A bulbous root vegetable with light brown skin and crisp, crunchy flesh. It is peeled and eaten raw or cooked.

OKRA: A tapered, oblong green pod with ridged skin. When cooked, okra gives off a thick, viscous liquid that acts as a thickening agent for soups and sauces.

ORZO: A small rice-shaped pasta.

PECORINO CHEESE: An Italian aged cheese made from sheep's milk.

PERCIATELLI (BUCATINI): A long, thick, tubular pasta.

PIMIENTO: A red sweet pepper.

POBLANO CHILE PEPPER: A mild dark green pepper popular in Mexican cuisine and often used for stuffing. When dried, poblanos are called anchos.

SAFFRON: The yellow-orange, aromatic stigmas of the small purple crocus, used to color and flavor many dishes. Saffron is the world's most expensive spice—it takes fourteen thousand laboriously collected and processed stigmas to make an ounce of saffron—but a little goes a long way and the result is delicious.

SHIITAKE MUSHROOMS: A wild mushroom that is now cultivated in the United States. It has a dark brown cap with a meaty, earthy flavor and can be found fresh or dried.

TOFU (SOY BEAN CURD, BEAN CURD): Tofu is made from curdled soy milk and is an excellent source of protein.

TURMERIC: A spice that gives an intense yellow color to food. It is the ground root of a tropical plant related to ginger and has a bitter, pungent flavor.

VALENCIA RICE: A medium-grain Spanish rice that is used in paella and other Spanish dishes. Valencia rice is grown in the United States and is available in most supermarkets.

FLAVORS OF THE

MEDITER- RANEAN

[PICTURED: *Tabbouleh and Toasted Walnut Couscous, page 54*]

EGGPLANT PARMESAN
with QUICK BROWN RICE

C
O
U
N
T
D
O
W
N

❶ Preheat broiler.
❷ Place water for rice on to boil.
❸ Prepare ingredients for eggplant recipe.
❹ Cook rice.
❺ Make eggplant recipe.

SHOPPING LIST

1 small bunch fresh basil

2 medium eggplants
(1½ pounds)

One 16-ounce container
low-fat ricotta cheese
(9 ounces needed)

Two 16-ounce cans
low-salt tomato sauce

One 14-ounce box
quick cooking brown rice

STAPLES

Garlic

Red onions (2)

Hot pepper sauce

Fresh Parmesan cheese

Olive oil

Olive oil spray

Salt

Black peppercorns

SERVES 4
This meal contains
664 calories per serving,
with 19 percent
of calories from fat.

his is a quick version of an old Italian favorite. Cutting the eggplant into small chunks helps it to cook and absorb the sauce flavor in only twenty minutes. Brown rice usually takes about forty-five minutes to one hour to cook. Use parboiled brown rice, which cuts the time in half, or use the ten-minute brown rice that is now available.

EGGPLANT PARMESAN

Olive oil spray

2 medium eggplants, unpeeled, cut into
2 x ½-inch-thick chunks (1½ pounds)

2 medium red onions, diced (4 cups)

6 medium cloves garlic, crushed

Two 16-ounce cans low-salt tomato sauce
(4 cups)

Several drops of hot pepper sauce

2 cups low-fat ricotta cheese

½ cup freshly grated Parmesan cheese

Salt and freshly ground black pepper to taste

½ cup fresh basil, chopped

Preheat broiler. Use a large nonstick frying
pan with an ovenproof handle, or use an
ovenproof wok. Prepare pan with olive oil
spray and place on high heat. When frying
pan is hot, brown eggplant on all sides, 3 to
4 minutes. Add onion and garlic and continue to sauté 5 minutes. Add tomato sauce
and hot pepper sauce. Bring to a simmer,
lower heat, cover, and cook 10 minutes.
Meanwhile, mix ricotta cheese and
Parmesan together in a medium-sized bowl.
When sauce is ready, remove it from heat
and add salt and pepper to taste. Spoon
cheese mixture evenly over sauce and place
pan under broiler 3 minutes. Remove from
broiler, sprinkle with basil, and serve over
brown rice.

QUICK BROWN RICE

2 cups quick-cooking brown rice

2 teaspoons olive oil

Salt and freshly ground black pepper to taste

Bring a large saucepan with 3 to 4 quarts
water to a boil. Place rice in a strainer and
rinse. When the water boils, stir in rice,
return to a boil, and boil rapidly, uncovered, 20 minutes, or follow package
instructions. Drain rice in a colander, leaving about ¼ cup water in saucepan. Mix
the oil into the water and return rice to
saucepan. Toss well. Add salt and pepper
to taste.

HELPFUL HINTS

➤ *Look for quick-cooking brown rice in the super-market.*

➤ *If low-salt tomato sauce is unavailable, use any type of tomato sauce.*

➤ *Buy good-quality Parmesan cheese and ask your grocer to grate it for you, or cut it into small pieces and chop it in the food processor. You can freeze freshly grated cheese for quick use with no loss of flavor.*

➤ *Use a large frying pan or casserole that can be used on the stovetop and placed under the broiler for a few minutes.*

ORZO AND THREE-CHEESE "RISOTTO"
with TOMATO AND ONION SALAD

SHOPPING LIST

One 10-ounce package
prewashed lettuce
(4 ounces needed)

2 ripe medium tomatoes
(1 pound)

4 ounces feta cheese, crumbled
(⅔ cup)

One 8-ounce container
nonfat ricotta cheese
(4½ ounces needed)

One 16-ounce package orzo
(8 ounces needed)

1 small package saffron strands

STAPLES

Red onion

Dijon mustard

Fresh Parmesan cheese

Skim milk

Vegetable broth
(three 14½-ounce cans)

Olive oil

Red wine vinegar

Cayenne pepper

Salt

Black peppercorns

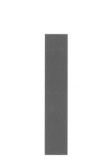

SERVES 4
This meal contains
529 calories per serving,
with 25 percent
of calories from fat.

created this recipe thinking it would make a quick substitute for baked macaroni. It turned out so creamy that it reminded me of an Italian risotto, but it's much easier to make.

ORZO AND THREE-CHEESE "RISOTTO"

4 cups vegetable broth

1 teaspoon saffron strands

½ medium red onion, diced (1 cup)

4 ounces feta cheese, crumbled (⅔ cup)

2 cups uncooked orzo

½ cup nonfat ricotta cheese

¼ cup skim milk

¼ cup freshly grated Parmesan cheese

¼ teaspoon cayenne pepper

Salt and freshly ground black pepper to taste

Bring broth and saffron to a boil in a large nonstick saucepan. Add onion, feta cheese, and orzo. Return to a boil and cook, uncovered, 5 minutes, stirring occasionally. Meanwhile, in a medium-sized bowl, mix ricotta cheese, milk, Parmesan cheese, and cayenne together. Test orzo to make sure it is cooked thoroughly and cook another minute or two if necessary. Stir in the ricotta mixture and adjust seasoning. Add salt sparingly; the Parmesan and feta may have provided enough salt. Add black pepper to taste.

TOMATO AND ONION SALAD

¼ cup diced red onion

¼ cup red wine vinegar

2 tablespoons Dijon mustard

¼ cup vegetable broth

2 teaspoons olive oil

Salt and freshly ground black pepper to taste

2 ripe medium tomatoes, washed and cut into eighths

4 ounces prewashed lettuce (2 cups)

Whisk onion, vinegar, and mustard together in a salad bowl. Add broth, oil, and a pinch of salt and pepper and whisk to combine. Add lettuce and tomato to bowl and toss with dressing.

HELPFUL HINTS

➤ *Crumbled feta cheese can be found in the dairy section of the supermarket.*

➤ *Buy good-quality Parmesan cheese and ask your grocer to grate it for you, or cut it into small pieces and chop it in the food processor. You can freeze freshly grated cheese for quick use with no loss of flavor.*

➤ *Turmeric or bijol may be substituted for saffron in the orzo dish.*

➤ *Onion is used in both recipes. Dice all at once and use as needed.*

➤ *Orzo tends to stick to the bottom of the pan. Use a nonstick pan, or scrape the bottom several times during cooking.*

FRITTATA PRIMAVERA
with GRATINÉED FENNEL

COUNTDOWN

❶ Preheat broiler.

❷ Prepare and begin cooking potatoes for frittata.

❸ Boil water for fennel.

❹ While potatoes cook, prepare vegetables for frittata.

❺ While frittata cooks, prepare fennel.

❻ Complete frittata.

SHOPPING LIST

1 small bunch fresh basil

1 medium fennel bulb (½ pound)

1 medium green bell pepper

¼ pound portobello mushrooms

1 pound red potatoes

1 loaf Italian bread

STAPLES

Garlic

Red onion

Butter or margarine

Fresh Parmesan cheese (4 ounces needed)

Large eggs (6)

Skim milk

Plain bread crumbs

Salt

Black peppercorns

SERVES 4

This meal contains 629 calories per serving, with 28 percent of calories from fat.

This is a light, quick supper, perfect for a busy weekday meal. Frittata Primavera ("spring style") is an Italian omelet filled with fresh vegetables. The secret is to cook it slowly for 10 minutes so that it becomes thick, more like a quiche than an omelet. Use fresh basil and good-quality fresh Parmesan cheese for the best results. I buy a large chunk of Parmigiano-Reggiano and either ask the grocer to grate it for me or I grate it in my food processor and freeze the extra for later use. ¶ Fennel, sometimes called anise, is a pale green bulb with feathery leaves similar to dill. It has a lightly sweet licorice flavor when raw and a pleasant, very mild flavor when cooked.

FRITTATA PRIMAVERA

1 pound red potatoes, unpeeled, diced
    (3 cups)
2 tablespoons butter or margarine
Salt and freshly ground black pepper to taste
1 medium red onion, sliced (2 cups)
¼ pound portobello mushrooms, sliced
    (1½ cups)
1 medium green bell pepper, sliced (1 cup)
4 medium cloves garlic, crushed
2 large whole eggs
4 large egg whites
½ cup skim milk
1 cup fresh basil
1 loaf Italian bread
Olive oil spray
½ cup freshly grated Parmesan cheese

Preheat broiler. Melt butter in a large
nonstick frying pan on medium-high heat.
Add potatoes, spreading cubes in a single
layer, and sauté. Toss to brown all sides,
about 5 minutes. Add a little salt and pepper
as potatoes cook. Meanwhile, prepare
onions, mushrooms, green pepper, and
garlic. Add to frying pan and sauté another
5 minutes. In a bowl, whisk whole eggs,
egg whites, and skim milk together. Tear
basil into small pieces and add to egg mixture with a little salt and pepper. Pour egg
mixture into frying pan and gently toss
vegetables to spread egg mixture throughout the pan. Turn heat to low and cook 10
minutes. Frittata will be mostly cooked
through. Sprinkle Parmesan on top and
place frittata under broiler when fennel is
finished cooking. Broil 2 minutes. While
frittata is in broiler, warm bread in broiler
under the frittata pan or place it in the
oven. To serve, loosen frittata around
edges, cut into quarters, and serve each
quarter on individual plates. Serve with
warm bread.

GRATINÉED FENNEL

1 medium fennel bulb, sliced (4 cups)
Salt and freshly ground black pepper to taste
¼ cup plain bread crumbs
½ cup freshly grated Parmesan cheese

Place a medium-sized pot of water on to
boil. Remove feathery top of fennel and
discard any outer leaves that look damaged.
Wash and slice bulb. Place in boiling water,
cover, and boil 5 minutes. Drain fennel in a
colander and spoon it into a 9 x 10-inch
baking dish. Sprinkle with salt and pepper
to taste. Mix bread crumbs and Parmesan
cheese together and sprinkle over fennel.
Place under broiler to brown, about 2
minutes.

HELPFUL HINTS

➤ *Use fresh thyme, dill,*
   or parsley if basil is
   unavailable.

➤ *An egg substitute can be*
   used instead of the whole
   egg and 2 egg whites.

➤ *Use a nonstick frying pan*
   with an ovenproof handle.

PASTA-STUFFED TOMATOES *with* ITALIAN WHITE BEAN SALAD

C
O
U
N
T
D
O
W
N

❶ Place water for pasta on to boil.
❷ Preheat oven to 350 degrees F to warm bread.
❸ Make tomatoes.
❹ Make bean salad.

SHOPPING LIST

2 small bunches fresh mint
1 medium red bell pepper
1 small head romaine lettuce
4 ripe medium tomatoes (2 pounds)
One 19-ounce can cannellini beans (white kidney beans)
One 16-ounce box acini pepe, alphabets, or orzo (4 ounces needed)
1 French baguette

STAPLES

Garlic
Lemon
Red onion
Fresh Parmesan cheese (One 2-ounce piece needed)
Olive oil
Dried rosemary
Dried sage
Salt
Black peppercorns

SERVES 4

This meal contains 608 calories per serving, with 25 percent of calories from fat.

With the use of a food processor, you can make this dinner in the time it takes to boil water and cook pasta. Large, juicy red tomatoes, perfect for stuffing, are filled with a quick pasta flavored with a pesto dressing. A simple white bean salad completes the meal. To speed things up, the tomato pulp and liquid is used as the base for the dressings in both recipes. If you have very juicy tomatoes, you will have more tomato liquid than is needed. Reserve any extra tomato liquid and add it to mayonnaise or yogurt for a quick salad dressing, or add it to soups or sauces for extra flavor.

32

PASTA-STUFFED TOMATOES

⅔ cup uncooked small pasta
   (acini pepe, alphabets, or orzo)

4 ripe medium tomatoes

¼ cup chopped red onion

2 tablespoons fresh lemon juice

1½ tablespoons olive oil

Salt and freshly ground black pepper to taste

2 cups chopped fresh mint

3 medium cloves garlic

¼ cup freshly grated Parmesan cheese

Bring a pot filled with 3 to 4 quarts water to a boil. Add pasta and cook, uncovered, 10 minutes. Meanwhile, remove stems from tomatoes, wash, and cut in half. Take a small slice off the bottom of each half so that it sits upright. With a serrated knife, cut around the inside edges and remove pulp and seeds, leaving the shell intact. Chop pulp in food processor or by hand. Remove to a bowl. Measure 1½ cups pulp and return to bowl of food processor, or to a separate bowl if mixing by hand. Add onion, lemon juice, and olive oil and mix well. Add salt and pepper to taste. Remove ¾ cup sauce and reserve for bean salad. Add mint, garlic, and Parmesan cheese to bowl and process, or mix just until smooth. Drain pasta in a colander, place in a bowl, and mix with sauce. Add more salt and pepper, if desired. Spoon stuffing into 8 tomato halves and place on a serving platter, leaving space in the center for the bean salad.

 ITALIAN WHITE BEAN SALAD
recipe follows

FLAVORS OF THE

MEDITER-RANEAN

HELPFUL HINTS

➤ *Red, yellow, or green bell pepper may be used.*

➤ *Red kidney beans may be substituted for the cannellini beans.*

➤ *Large curls of fresh Parmesan garnish the bean salad and freshly grated Parmesan is used in the pasta stuffing. Buy the Parmesan in a block and shave off several curls with a potato peeler. Grate the rest for the stuffing.*

➤ *If you plan ahead, you can chop everything in the food processor without having to wash the bowl. Grate dry ingredients such as Parmesan first, then chop the mint. Chop the onion next and purée the tomato pulp.*

ITALIAN WHITE BEAN SALAD

½ small head romaine lettuce (2 cups)

¾ cup tomato sauce reserved from
  Pasta-Stuffed Tomato recipe

4 teaspoons olive oil

2 medium cloves garlic, crushed

1 teaspoon dried rosemary

1 teaspoon dried sage

2 cups canned cannellini beans
  (white kidney beans), drained and rinsed

1 medium red bell pepper, cut into bean-sized
  pieces (1 cup)

Salt and freshly ground black pepper to taste

2 tablespoons freshly shaved Parmesan cheese

1 French baguette

Preheat oven to 350 degrees F and warm bread in oven for 5 minutes. Wash and dry lettuce. Tear into bite-sized pieces and arrange in the center of the serving platter. Pour reserved tomato sauce over lettuce. Heat oil in a medium-sized sauté pan. Add garlic and herbs and sauté 1 minute on medium-low heat. Remove from heat. Add beans and red bell pepper and toss in the hot pan to coat with herbs and garlic. Add salt and pepper to taste. Spoon bean salad over lettuce. Using a potato peeler, shave Parmesan over beans. Serve with warm French baguette.

FLAVORS OF THE

MEDITER-
RANEAN

PICTURED:

*Pasta-Stuffed Tomatoes with
Italian White Bean Salad*

ROASTED RED PEPPER PASTA *with* SAUTÉED ESCAROLE AND CHICKPEAS

C O U N T D O W N

❶ Preheat broiler.
❷ Make pasta sauce.
❸ Cook pasta and toss with sauce.
❹ Make sautéed escarole and chickpeas.

SHOPPING LIST

2 small heads escarole
4 medium red bell peppers
One 15½-ounce can chickpeas
One 10¾-ounce can tomato purée
One 16-ounce box fusilli

STAPLES

Garlic
Olive oil
Olive oil spray
Salt
Black peppercorns

SERVES 4
This meal contains 638 calories per serving, with 14 percent of calories from fat.

Dinner at my friend Jacques Pepin's home is always special. One evening Jacques served a red pepper sauce over homemade ravioli. When he told me how easy it was to make the sauce, I decided to use it as a basis for this quick dinner. The sauce is puréed in a food processor or blender. If you don't have either machine, mix together all of the ingredients after the peppers have been sautéed. The sauce will still be delicious; it will simply have a chunky rather than a smooth texture. ¶ Fusilli corti (short springs or corkscrews) is best in this dish, as the ridges in the pasta trap the sauce, adding to the texture and flavor, but any short pasta, such as penne or elbow macaroni, can be used.

ROASTED RED PEPPER PASTA

Olive oil spray
4 medium red bell peppers
2 medium cloves garlic
2 teaspoons olive oil
1 cup canned tomato purée
Salt and freshly ground black pepper to taste
16 ounces uncooked fusilli

Preheat broiler. Bring a large saucepan filled with 3 to 4 quarts water to a boil. Line a baking tray with aluminum foil. Spray red bell peppers with olive oil spray and place peppers and garlic on tray. Place tray in broiler 5 minutes, remove and turn peppers and garlic, and broil 5 minutes more. Remove tray from broiler and let cool. Slice peppers open and remove seeds and stems. Place peppers, garlic, olive oil, and tomato purée in a food processor or blender and blend until smooth. Add salt and pepper to taste. When water is boiling, add pasta and boil 10 minutes. Drain in a colander and toss with sauce.

SAUTÉED ESCAROLE AND CHICKPEAS

2 teaspoons olive oil
4 medium cloves garlic, crushed
One 15½-ounce can chickpeas, drained and rinsed (1½ cups)
2 small heads escarole, sliced in 2-inch strips
Salt and freshly ground black pepper to taste

Heat oil in a large nonstick frying pan on high heat. Add garlic and chickpeas and sauté 1 minute. Add escarole to frying pan and sauté 3 minutes. Add salt and pepper to taste.

FLAVORS OF THE
MEDITER-RANEAN

HELPFUL HINTS

➤ *Any firm lettuce, such as romaine, can be substituted for escarole.*

➤ *Crushed garlic is used in both recipes. Crush all at once and use as needed.*

➤ *Escarole, like spinach, uses a lot of pan space before it cooks down. If you don't have a large nonstick frying pan, you can use a large nonstick saucepan.*

➤ *To save clean-up time, when pasta sauce is done, sauté the escarole in the same frying pan without washing it.*

PERCIATELLI AND BROCCOLI *with* FENNEL AND ORANGE SALAD

COUNTDOWN

❶ Place water for pasta on to boil.
❷ Make pasta dish.
❸ While pasta is cooking, make salad.

SHOPPING LIST

I small bunch fresh basil
I pound broccoli florets
I medium fennel bulb
(½ pound)
2 medium oranges
One 5½-ounce jar
pitted green olives
I small package pecorino cheese
(I ounce needed)
Three 14½-ounce cans whole
tomatoes (36 ounces needed)
One 16-ounce box perciatelli
One 1¾-ounce jar pine nuts
(I ounce needed)

STAPLES

Garlic
Yellow onion
Raisins
Olive oil
Salt
Black peppercorns

SERVES 4
This meal contains
759 calories per serving,
with 23 percent
of calories from fat.

For years, Northern Italian cuisine has captured the spotlight, but Sicilian cooking is lately coming back into vogue. With vegetables, pasta, fish, and bread as its staples, it fits right in with today's ideas about good food. ¶ Perciatelli, also called bucatini, is a long, thick, tubular pasta that adds texture and flavor to this Sicilian dish. Fennel, popular in Italian cuisine, is available year-round. It has a bulb base with feathery stems, a texture similar to celery, and a flavor reminiscent of anise or licorice. Served with slices of orange, it makes a wonderfully refreshing salad. The dish is garnished with pecorino, a hard country cheese made from sheep's milk. Pecorino, with its hard, grainy texture and sharp flavor, is similar to Parmesan cheese but is aged for a much shorter time.

PERCIATELLI AND BROCCOLI

1 pound broccoli florets

2 teaspoons olive oil

1 medium yellow onion, sliced (2 cups)

2 medium cloves garlic, crushed

4 cups canned whole tomatoes, including liquid

Salt and freshly ground black pepper to taste

¼ cup raisins

¼ cup pine nuts

16 pitted green olives, cut in half

1 pound uncooked perciatelli

6 sprigs fresh basil, chopped (about ½ cup)

⅓ cup freshly grated pecorino cheese

Place a large pot with 3 to 4 quarts of water on to boil. In a second saucepan, cook broccoli in boiling water for 5 minutes, or place in microwave oven on "high" for 6 minutes. Drain in a colander and set aside. Heat oil in a large nonstick frying pan on medium heat. Add onion and garlic and sauté until soft, about 5 minutes. Add tomatoes, cutting them in half in the pan with a spoon. Add salt and pepper to taste. Cover and simmer 15 minutes.

Add raisins, pine nuts, olives, and broccoli, cover, and simmer 5 minutes more. Meanwhile, add pasta to boiling water and return to a boil. Cook 11 minutes, or until pasta is cooked through but firm. Drain in a colander and place in a serving dish. Pour sauce over pasta and toss well. Chop fresh basil leaves and mix in. Sprinkle pecorino cheese on top. Serve immediately.

 FENNEL AND ORANGE SALAD
recipe follows

HELPFUL HINTS

➤ *Use ziti if perciatelli is unavailable.*

➤ *Use freshly grated Parmesan cheese if pecorino is unavailable.*

➤ *Celery can be substituted for fennel in the salad.*

➤ *Buy ready-to-use broccoli florets.*

FENNEL AND ORANGE SALAD

1 medium fennel bulb, sliced (4 cups)
2 medium oranges
2 tablespoons fresh orange juice
1 tablespoon olive oil
Salt to taste

Remove stalk, any brown or damaged leaves, and the green stem from fennel bulb, cut in quarters, and slice. Over a bowl, peel and cut oranges into 1- to 2-inch cubes, preserving as much juice as possible. To peel the oranges quickly, cut off the top and, using a sawing motion, cut the skin away from the flesh, circling the fruit. Measure 2 tablespoons juice and discard the rest. Slice oranges in ¼-inch-thick circles and add to bowl. Add the 2 tablespoons juice and add the olive oil. Mix well. Add salt to taste. Add fennel and toss again. Serve on salad plates to accompany pasta.

FLAVORS OF THE
MEDITER-RANEAN

PICTURED:

Perciatelli and Broccoli with Fennel and Orange Salad

WILD MUSHROOM RISOTTO
with CREAMED SPINACH

C O U N T D O W N

❶ Start risotto.
❷ While making risotto, prepare spinach and set aside.
❸ Finish risotto.

SHOPPING LIST

1 small bunch fresh parsley

¾ pound portobello, oyster, or porcini mushrooms

Two 10-ounce packages fresh prewashed spinach, or 20 ounces frozen whole-leaf spinach

One 8-ounce container light cream (2 ounces needed)

One 14-ounce package arborio or Valencia rice

STAPLES

Garlic

Red onions (2)

Fresh Parmesan cheese

Vegetable broth (one 14½-ounce can)

All-purpose flour

Olive oil

Dry white wine

Ground nutmeg

Salt

Black peppercorns

SERVES 4

This meal contains 833 calories per serving, with 15 percent of calories from fat.

isotto, a flavorful Italian rice dish, is simple to make, but you do need to stir frequently while it cooks, about 20 minutes. This unique method of cooking allows the rice to absorb enough hot broth to swell and become creamy, yet each grain remains firm. In this recipe, the cooking time is shortened by using a nonstick frying pan instead of a saucepan. The wider base of the frying pan allows more grains of rice to be in direct contact with the heat. A nonstick pan also allows you to let the rice cook on its own for 2 or 3 minutes at a time without it sticking. The best type of rice to use is a medium-grain Italian arborio rice. If this is difficult to find, you can use a short-grain Valencia rice with delicious results, even though it is not an authentic risotto.

WILD MUSHROOM RISOTTO

2 cups vegetable broth
2 cups dry white wine
2 cups water
2 tablespoons olive oil, divided
1 medium red onion, sliced (2 cups)
2 medium cloves garlic, crushed
¾ pound portobello, oyster, or porcini
  mushrooms, sliced (8 cups)
2 cups uncooked arborio or Valencia rice
½ cup freshly grated Parmesan cheese
1 cup chopped fresh parsley
Salt and freshly ground black pepper to taste

In a large saucepan, combine broth, wine,
and water, and bring to a simmer. (Or heat
in a large bowl in a microwave oven on
"high" for 3 minutes.) Heat 1 tablespoon
oil in a large nonstick frying pan on medium heat. Add onion and garlic and sauté
2 minutes. Add mushrooms and sauté
another 2 minutes. Add rice and continue
to sauté 1 minute. Pour in 1 cup liquid.
Continue to cook over medium heat, stirring every few minutes. As the rice absorbs
the liquid, add a little more. Continue to
stir and add more liquid as needed. After
20 minutes, most of the liquid will be
absorbed. Remove from heat and stir in
remaining olive oil, Parmesan cheese, and
parsley. Add salt and pepper to taste.

CREAMED SPINACH

½ cup water
½ medium red onion, sliced (1 cup)
20 ounces prewashed spinach (16 cups)
3 tablespoons all-purpose flour
¼ cup light cream
Pinch of nutmeg
Salt and freshly ground black pepper to taste

Heat water in a large nonstick saucepan on
medium heat. Add onion and sauté 3 minutes. Add spinach, cover, and cook 10 minutes. If any liquid is left in the pan, remove
cover, raise heat, and cook to evaporate the
liquid. Break up spinach with the edge of a
cooking spoon. Add flour and toss with
spinach. Add cream, nutmeg, and salt and
pepper to taste. Mix well.

FLAVORS OF THE
MEDITER-RANEAN

HELPFUL HINTS

➤ *Portobello, oyster, porcini, or other types of wild mushrooms may be used.*

➤ *Buy good-quality Parmesan cheese and ask your grocer to grate it for you, or cut it into small pieces and chop it in the food processor. You can freeze freshly grated cheese for quick use with no loss of flavor.*

➤ *Onion is used in both recipes. Slice all at once and use as needed.*

➤ *Use a microwave oven to warm broth and wine.*

➤ *The amount of liquid needed may vary. The rice should be creamy, not runny. Add all of the liquid only if needed. If the rice is dry but not thoroughly cooked, add a little water and cook longer.*

STUFFED SHELLS
with HERBED ZUCCHINI

COUNTDOWN

❶ Place water for shells on to boil.
❷ Preheat broiler.
❸ Make stuffed shells.
❹ Make zucchini.

SHOPPING LIST

2 medium oranges

1 small bunch fresh parsley

1 pound zucchini

1 small package
crumbled gorgonzola cheese
(2 ounces needed)

1 small piece pecorino cheese
(1 ounce needed)

One 16-ounce container
nonfat ricotta cheese

Two 28-ounce cans crushed
tomatoes (36 ounces needed)

One 12-ounce box
jumbo pasta shells

One 2½-ounce package walnut
pieces (1½ ounces needed)

STAPLES

Garlic

Yellow onion

Olive oil

Dried rosemary

Sugar

Salt

Black peppercorns

SERVES 4
This meal contains
616 calories per serving,
with 28 percent
of the calories from fat.

orgonzola cheese and walnuts add a rich flavor to these stuffed shells. The shells will last several days in the refrigerator and can be frozen. The secret to this sauce is the grated orange rind (zest). To get the most flavor, grate the rind directly over the sauce; the spray will be captured in the sauce. Freeze the sauce separately from the shells to keep them from becoming soggy.

STUFFED SHELLS

24 uncooked jumbo pasta shells

TOMATO SAUCE

4 cups canned crushed tomatoes
1 medium yellow onion, sliced (2 cups)
4 medium cloves garlic, crushed
Grated zest from 2 oranges
1 teaspoon sugar (optional)
Salt and freshly ground black pepper to taste

STUFFING

2 cups nonfat ricotta cheese
⅓ cup crumbled gorgonzola cheese
⅔ cup chopped fresh parsley
⅓ cup walnut pieces
¼ cup grated pecorino cheese

Bring a large pot filled with 3 to 4 quarts water to a boil. Add shells and boil 10 minutes. Place tomatoes, onion, and garlic in a medium-sized saucepan. Grate orange zest over sauce. Simmer, covered, 10 minutes. Taste and add sugar, if needed. Add salt and pepper to taste. To make the stuffing, mix together ricotta, gorgonzola, parsley, and walnuts. Drain shells in a colander and let cool a few minutes.

Fill each shell with stuffing and place in a 13 x 9–inch ovenproof serving dish or on a baking tray in a single layer. Spoon sauce over top and sprinkle with pecorino cheese. Place in broiler 5 minutes. Remove and cover with aluminum foil until you are ready to serve.

 HERBED ZUCCHINI
recipe follows

HELPFUL HINTS

➤ *Domestic crumbled gorgonzola can be found in most supermarkets.*

➤ *Any type of blue cheese can be used.*

➤ *Parmesan can be substituted for pecorino cheese.*

➤ *Crushed garlic is used in both recipes. Crush all at once and use as needed.*

➤ *The stuffed shells and zucchini both cook in the broiler for the same amount of time. If your broiler is big enough, cook them at the same time. Otherwise, cook the shells and then the zucchini.*

➤ *If pressed for time, use a bottled spaghetti sauce.*

HERBED ZUCCHINI

1 pound zucchini, thinly sliced (4 cups)
¼ cup water
2 teaspoons olive oil
2 medium cloves garlic, crushed
2 teaspoons dried rosemary
Salt and freshly ground black pepper to taste

Preheat boiler. Line a baking tray with aluminum foil. Mix water, olive oil, garlic, and rosemary together in a small bowl. Add zucchini and toss to combine. Spoon zucchini and sauce in one layer on baking tray. Place in broiler about 5 inches from heat. Cook 5 minutes. Add salt and pepper to taste. Remove and serve with stuffed shells.

FLAVORS OF THE
MEDITER-RANEAN

PICTURED:

*Stuffed Shells with
Herbed Zucchini*

47

GREEK PASTA *with* LEMON VINAIGRETTE SALAD

C
O
U
N
T
D
O
W
N

❶ Place water for pasta on to boil.
❷ Make pasta sauce.
❸ Prepare salad.
❹ Finish pasta.

SHOPPING LIST

1 medium cucumber
1 medium green bell pepper
1 small bunch radishes
1 small head romaine lettuce
1 small bunch scallions
1 small bunch fresh oregano, or dried oregano
1 small bunch fresh thyme, or dried thyme
4 ripe medium tomatoes (2 pounds)
4 ounces feta cheese, crumbled
1 pound fresh linguine

STAPLES

Garlic
Lemons (3)
Red onion
Dijon mustard
Olive oil
Olive oil spray
Salt
Black peppercorns

SERVES 4
This meal contains 582 calories per serving, with 24 percent of calories from fat.

Cross-cultural cooking has resulted in the creation of some interesting tastes and textures. In this dish, feta cheese, lemon juice, oregano, thyme, and fresh vegetables combine with olive oil and pasta for a Greek/Italian–influenced flavor combination. Crisp lettuce, cucumbers, and radishes form the basis of a good Greek salad. To this, any number of vegetables can be added. Add whatever vegetables are available or look best in the market.

GREEK PASTA

Olive oil spray

½ medium red onion, diced (1 cup)

1 medium green bell pepper, diced (1 cup)

4 medium cloves garlic, crushed

4 ripe medium tomatoes, diced (4 cups)

Salt and freshly ground black pepper to taste

1 pound uncooked fresh linguine

2 tablespoons fresh thyme,
 or 2 teaspoons dried

4 tablespoons fresh oregano, or
 4 teaspoons dried

4 ounces feta cheese, crumbled (⅔ cup)

4 teaspoons olive oil

4 tablespoons fresh lemon juice

Place 2 to 3 quarts water on to boil for pasta. Prepare a medium-sized nonstick frying pan with olive oil spray and place on high heat. When frying pan is hot, sauté onions, green bell pepper, and garlic 3 to 4 minutes. Add tomatoes and sauté 2 minutes. Remove from heat and pour into a serving bowl. Add salt and pepper to taste. When water boils, add pasta and cook 3 minutes (if using dried pasta, cook 9 minutes). Drain pasta in a colander and toss with sauce. Add herbs and feta cheese and toss again. In a small bowl, mix olive oil and lemon juice together and pour over pasta. Toss well, add salt and pepper to taste, and serve.

LEMON VINAIGRETTE SALAD

LEMON VINAIGRETTE

2 tablespoons fresh lemon juice

2 teaspoons Dijon mustard

4 tablespoons water

2 teaspoons olive oil

Salt and freshly ground black pepper to taste

SALAD

½ head romaine lettuce (2 cups)

1 medium cucumber, sliced

4 scallions, sliced (⅔ cup)

8 radishes, sliced

8 slices red onion

In a medium-sized salad bowl, whisk lemon juice and mustard together. Add water and oil and blend well. Add salt and pepper to taste. Wash, dry, and tear lettuce into bite-sized pieces. Place in bowl and add cucumber, scallions, radishes, and onion. Toss well. Add salt and pepper to taste.

HELPFUL HINTS

➤ *If pressed for time, use a bottled low-fat vinaigrette for the salad.*

➤ *Fresh herbs are available year-round in most supermarkets; use them if you can. If using dried herbs, be sure they are no older than six months.*

➤ *Dried linguine can be used if fresh linguine is unavailable.*

MIDDLE EASTERN COUSCOUS SALAD *with* CHAKCHOUKA (A TUNISIAN COOKED TOMATO AND PEPPER SALAD)

C
O
U
N
T
D
O
W
N

❶ Preheat broiler.
❷ Start caramelizing onions for couscous, then measure remaining ingredients.
❸ Boil water for couscous.
❹ Make Chakchouka.
❺ Complete couscous salad while Chakchouka simmers.

SHOPPING LIST

One 8-ounce package dried cranberries (4 ounces needed)
1 small bunch fresh mint
2 medium red bell peppers
2 ripe medium tomatoes (1 pound)
1 medium zucchini (½ pound)
One 15-ounce can chickpeas
One 10-ounce package couscous (4 ounces needed)
4 pita breads

STAPLES

Carrots
Fresh orange juice
Garlic
Yellow onion
Dijon mustard
Olive oil
Olive oil spray
Distilled white vinegar
Cayenne pepper
Ground cinnamon
Sugar
Salt
Black peppercorns

SERVES 4
This meal contains 659 calories per serving, with 23 percent of calories from fat.

Refreshing mint, garlic, raisins, and orange juice give this couscous salad a hint of the Middle East. Couscous is a form of pasta, made by moistening hard durum wheat and rolling it in flour to form tiny pellets. An authentic Moroccan couscous takes about an hour to make. Precooked couscous, the kind found in most supermarkets, takes only 5 minutes to make. ¶ Chakchouka, a Mediterranean cooked tomato salad, can also be made with hard-boiled eggs. The pita bread can be served warm or at room temperature.

MIDDLE EASTERN COUSCOUS SALAD

3 tablespoons olive oil, divided

½ medium yellow onion, sliced (1 cup)

1 cup water

⅔ cup uncooked couscous

2 large carrots, sliced (1 cup)

½ medium zucchini, cut into 1-inch dice (1 cup)

4 medium cloves garlic, crushed

1 cup dried cranberries

One 15½-ounce can chickpeas, drained (1½ cups)

⅓ cup distilled white vinegar

2 tablespoons Dijon mustard

⅓ cup fresh orange juice

¼ teaspoon cayenne pepper

½ teaspoon ground cinnamon

Salt and freshly ground black pepper to taste

½ cup coarsely chopped fresh mint, for garnish

Heat 1 tablespoon of oil in a large nonstick frying pan on medium heat. Add onion and sauté 10 minutes. Meanwhile, bring water to a boil in a medium-sized saucepan, remove from heat, and add couscous. Cover and let stand 5 minutes. Add carrots, zucchini, and garlic to pan and cook 10 minutes more. Place couscous in a large bowl and fluff with a fork. Add onion mixture, cranberries, and chickpeas and toss well. Mix vinegar and mustard together in a small bowl and stir in orange juice, remaining oil, cayenne, and cinnamon. Add this mixture to couscous and mix well. Add salt and pepper to taste. Place in a serving bowl or on individual plates and sprinkle mint on top.

✳ **CHAKCHOUKA**
recipe follows

HELPFUL HINTS

➤ *Any type of onion may be used for the salad. Yellow onion is called for because it has a stronger flavor than many other types.*

➤ *Crushed garlic is used in both recipes. Crush all at once and use as needed.*

➤ *Caramelizing the onions gives the salad a natural, sweet flavor. They take 20 minutes to cook, so start them first.*

➤ *To keep couscous fluffy, toss with a fork instead of a spoon.*

CHAKCHOUKA (A TUNISIAN COOKED TOMATO AND PEPPER SALAD)

2 medium red bell peppers

Olive oil spray

2 teaspoons olive oil

½ medium yellow onion, sliced (1 cup)

2 medium cloves garlic, crushed

2 ripe medium tomatoes, cut into wedges

1 teaspoon sugar

Salt and freshly ground black pepper to taste

4 pita breads

Preheat broiler. Line a baking tray with aluminum foil and place red bell peppers on tray. Spray peppers with olive oil spray. Broil 5 minutes per side. Heat oil in a medium-sized nonstick frying pan on medium-high heat. Add onion and garlic and sauté 5 minutes. Remove peppers from broiler, and core, seed, and slice them. Add peppers and tomatoes to frying pan. Simmer 15 minutes. If mixture is watery, cook a few minutes more. Sprinkle with sugar and toss well. Add salt and pepper to taste. Place pita in broiler, which should still be warm from cooking peppers, for 2 minutes before serving. Spoon warm salad into a serving bowl or on individual plates with couscous salad and serve with warm pita bread.

FLAVORS OF THE
MEDITER-RANEAN

PICTURED:

Middle Eastern Couscous Salad with Chakchouka

TABBOULEH *with* TOASTED WALNUT COUSCOUS

C O U N T D O W N

❶ Preheat oven to 350 degrees F.
❷ Soak bulgur wheat.
❸ Prepare ingredients for tabbouleh.
❹ Make couscous.
❺ Drain bulgur and finish tabbouleh.

SHOPPING LIST

1 large bunch fresh mint
1 small bunch fresh parsley
1 small bunch scallions
2 ripe medium tomatoes
(1 pound)
One 8-ounce jar
pitted black olives
One 6-ounce package
bulgur wheat (4 ounces needed)
One 10-ounce package couscous
(6 ounces needed)
One 2½-ounce package
walnut pieces (1 ounce needed)
4 pita breads

STAPLES

Lemons (2)
Tomato paste (6 ounces)
Vegetable broth
(one 14½-ounce can)
Olive oil
Salt
Black peppercorns

SERVES 4
This meal contains
669 calories per serving,
with 28 percent
of calories from fat.

*Y*ou can taste the bright sunshine and rich harvest of the Middle East in the refreshing flavors of fresh lemon juice, olive oil, lots of fresh mint, and parsley. Bulgur wheat, which adds an earthy flavor, is made from wheat kernels by steaming, drying, and crushing them. One secret to a flavorful tabbouleh is to crush the scallions and wheat together so that the juices from the scallions penetrate the wheat.

TABBOULEH

⅔ cup uncooked fine bulgur wheat

8 scallions, sliced (1½ cups)

1 cup chopped fresh parsley
(flat-leaf, if available)

1 cup chopped fresh mint

2 tablespoons olive oil

¼ cup fresh lemon juice

Salt and freshly ground black pepper to taste

2 ripe medium tomatoes, washed and
cut into eighths

8 pitted black olives, cut in quarters

4 pita breads

Preheat oven to 350 degrees F. Place bulgur wheat in a medium-sized bowl and add cold water to cover. Let stand 20 minutes. Drain and squeeze out as much moisture as possible with your hands. Add the scallions and squeeze again so that the scallion juices penetrate the wheat. Add parsley, mint, olive oil, and lemon juice and toss well. Add salt and pepper to taste. Spoon onto a serving plate and place tomatoes and olives on top. Warm pita bread in oven 5 minutes before serving.

TOASTED WALNUT COUSCOUS

1 cup tomato paste

⅔ cup vegetable broth

1 cup uncooked couscous

¼ cup walnut pieces

1 tablespoon olive oil

Salt and freshly ground black pepper to taste

Preheat oven to 350 degrees F. Combine tomato paste and broth in a medium-sized saucepan. Bring to a boil. Remove from heat. Add couscous, stir, cover, and let stand 5 minutes. Place walnuts on an aluminum foil–lined baking tray and toast in oven 10 minutes or in toaster oven 5 minutes, until brown. Meanwhile, add olive oil to the couscous and fluff with a fork to separate grains. Add salt and pepper to taste. Spoon onto a serving plate and sprinkle toasted walnuts on top.

HELPFUL HINTS

➤ *The bulgur wheat needs to soak in water for 20 minutes. While it soaks, prepare the rest of the meal.*

➤ *Toast walnuts in a toaster oven or in the same oven when warming pita bread.*

MODERN
AMERICAN
COMFORT FOODS

[PICTURED: *Stanley's Casserole Soup with Caramelized Shallot and Garlic Toast, page 66*]

ALL-AMERICAN PEPPER, MUSHROOM, AND ONION PIZZA *with* PANZANELLA SALAD (BREAD SALAD)

C O U N T D O W N

❶ Preheat oven to 400 degrees F.
❷ Make tomato sauce for pizza.
❸ Prepare remaining pizza ingredients.
❹ While pizza is in the oven, make panzanella salad.

SHOPPING LIST

1 small bunch fresh basil

1 medium cucumber

¼ pound mushrooms

2 medium red bell peppers

2 ripe medium tomatoes
(1 pound)

One 8-ounce package mozzarella cheese (6 ounces needed)

One 28-ounce can crushed tomatoes (18 ounces needed)

One 2-ounce jar capers
(4 tablespoons needed)

1 small loaf country bread

4 small precooked pizza bases or 2 large (12-inch) bases

STAPLES

Red onions (2)

Garlic

Lemon

Hot pepper sauce

Vegetable broth
(one 14½-ounce can)

Olive oil

Olive oil spray

Cayenne pepper

Salt

Black peppercorns

SERVES 4
This meal contains 715 calories per serving, with 30 percent of calories from fat.

Old-fashioned pizza-parlor pizza is regaining its popularity, and with good reason. Gourmet pizzas are delicious, but there's nothing like pizza topped with lots of extras. This pizza is ready quicker than it takes to order out. ¶ The crisp, cool panzanella salad, also known as "poor man's salad," provides a pleasant contrast to the hot pizza.

ALL-AMERICAN PEPPER, MUSHROOM, AND ONION PIZZA

SAUCE

2 cups canned crushed tomatoes

2 medium cloves garlic, crushed

Pinch of cayenne pepper

½ cup fresh basil

1 cup vegetable broth

1 medium red onion, sliced (2 cups)

2 medium red bell peppers, sliced (2 cups)

¼ pound mushrooms, sliced (1½ cups)

Olive oil spray

4 small precooked pizza bases, or 2 large
  (12-inch) bases

6 ounces mozzarella cheese, sliced (1 cup)

Salt and freshly ground black pepper to taste

Preheat oven to 400 degrees F. Purée all the sauce ingredients in a food processor, or chop basil by hand and mix in remaining sauce ingredients. Place vegetable broth in a medium-sized nonstick frying pan. Add onion and red bell peppers and sauté over medium-high heat until onions are golden, about 10 minutes. If pan becomes dry, add a little more stock or water to keep onions from burning. Add mushrooms and sauté about 3 minutes, or until soft. To assemble pizza, line a baking tray with aluminum foil and spray with olive oil spray. Place pizza bases on foil. Spoon tomato sauce over each base. Sprinkle vegetables evenly over the top and place sliced mozzarella cheese over vegetables. Place in hot oven until cheese is bubbly, 8 to 10 minutes.

PANZANELLA SALAD (BREAD SALAD)

4 tablespoons capers, drained and crushed

2 medium cloves garlic, crushed

1½ tablespoons olive oil, divided

1 tablespoon fresh lemon juice

Several drops hot pepper sauce

1 medium cucumber, diced (2 cups)

2 ripe medium tomatoes, diced (2 cups)

¼ cup sliced red onion

4 thick slices country bread

Preheat broiler. Blend capers and garlic together in a food processor. Add 1 tablespoon oil. Add lemon juice and hot pepper sauce and blend together. Remove and toss with cucumber, tomatoes, and onion in a serving bowl and set aside. (If mixing by hand, crush capers and garlic through a garlic press into a serving bowl. Add liquids and blend. Add vegetables and toss.) Brush bread with remaining oil. Place on a baking tray and broil 2 minutes, or until golden, or place in toaster oven and toast 2 minutes. Slice the bread into thick strips and place on individual plates. Spoon salad over bread.

MODERN
AMERICAN
COMFORT FOODS

HELPFUL HINTS

➤ *This uncooked tomato sauce recipe is fast and delicious. If you are very pressed for time, use your favorite bottled tomato sauce or pasta sauce.*

➤ *Buy good-quality Parmesan cheese and ask your grocer to grate it for you, or cut it into small pieces and chop it in the food processor. You can freeze freshly grated cheese for quick use with no loss of flavor.*

➤ *Buy ready-made pizza bases, or use French baguettes sliced in half lengthwise or English muffin halves.*

➤ *For the salad, crush the capers and garlic together with a metal garlic press.*

➤ *Onion is used in both recipes. Slice all at once and use as needed.*

RICOTTA SOUFFLÉ
with TOMATO BRUSCHETTA

COUNTDOWN

❶ Preheat oven to 400 degrees F to cook soufflé and toast bread.

❷ Make soufflé.

❸ Prepare bruschetta topping.

❹ Toast bread in the oven for a few minutes just before the soufflé is finished.

SHOPPING LIST

1 small bunch fresh basil

½ pound mushrooms

2 ripe medium tomatoes (1 pound)

1 medium zucchini (½ pound)

One 16-ounce container low-fat ricotta cheese (9 ounces needed)

1 French baguette

STAPLES

Carrots

Garlic

Red onion

Large eggs

Plain bread crumbs

Olive oil

Salt

Black peppercorns

SERVES 4
This meal contains 534 calories per serving, with 27 percent of calories from fat.

autéed vegetables mixed with ricotta cheese and topped with bread crumbs make this an unusual soufflé. The zucchini and carrots are grated and the mushrooms and onions are sliced, providing variety of texture. ¶ The soufflé only takes 20 minutes to make. Grating some of the vegetables helps the dish cook faster, and spreading the mixture in a thin layer in a baking dish cuts down baking time.

RICOTTA SOUFFLÉ

2 teaspoons olive oil

1 medium zucchini, grated (2 cups)

4 medium carrots, grated (2 cups)

½ pound mushrooms, sliced (3 cups)

½ medium red onion, sliced (1 cup)

½ cup chopped fresh basil

1 cup plain bread crumbs

Salt and freshly ground black pepper to taste

2 cups low-fat ricotta cheese

2 large whole eggs

Preheat oven to 400 degrees F. Heat oil in a large nonstick frying pan on medium heat. Add zucchini, carrots, mushrooms, and onion. Cover and cook 5 minutes.

Meanwhile, in a small bowl, mix basil with bread crumbs and add salt and pepper to taste. Set aside. Remove vegetables from heat, spoon into a 10 x 8–inch ovenproof dish or lasagna dish, add salt and pepper to taste, and spread out to cool. Mix the ricotta cheese and eggs together. Then combine the cheese mixture with the vegetables and spread evenly. Sprinkle bread crumb mixture on top. Bake 15 minutes.

TOMATO BRUSCHETTA

1 French baguette

1 medium clove garlic

2 ripe medium tomatoes, diced (2 cups)

2 teaspoons olive oil

Salt and freshly ground black pepper to taste

Line a baking tray with aluminum foil. Cut baguette in half lengthwise and cut into 5-inch slices. Place on tray and toast in oven until golden, 3 to 4 minutes. Remove from oven. Cut garlic clove in half and rub cut halves over bread. In a medium-sized bowl, toss diced tomato and olive oil together. Add salt and pepper to taste. Spoon mixture over baguette and serve.

MODERN
AMERICAN
COMFORT FOODS

HELPFUL HINTS

➤ *Any variety of vegetables can be substituted in this recipe; just make sure they are cooked through before adding the cheese.*

➤ *All of the vegetables can be prepared in 5 minutes using a food processor. Use the grating disk first for the zucchini and carrots. Remove vegetables to a bowl. Change to a slicing disk for the mushrooms and onions. Remove to bowl. Change to the chopping blade for the fresh basil. If you don't have a grating disk attachment, use a very thin slicing blade. The shape of the vegetables doesn't matter as long as they are thinly cut.*

➤ *The bruschetta can be made with any type of bread you have on hand.*

FRICASSÉE *with* FRENCH BRIE SALAD

C O U N T D O W N

❶ Preheat oven to 300 degrees F.
❷ Start lentils.
❸ Start fricassée.
❹ Make Brie salad.
❺ Finish fricassée.

SHOPPING LIST

One 10-ounce package pre-washed mesclun or baby lettuce (8 ounces needed)

1½ pounds shiitake mushrooms

1 small bunch fresh parsley

4 ounces Brie

Five 7½-ounce cans sliced red pimientos (32 ounces needed)

One 12-ounce package dried lentils (7 ounces needed)

1 small bottle walnut oil

One 2½-ounce package walnut pieces (1 ounce needed)

1 French baguette

STAPLES

Celery

Garlic

Lemons (2)

Red onion

Vegetable broth (one 14½-ounce can)

All-purpose flour

White basmati rice

Olive oil

Dry vermouth

Ground nutmeg

Salt

Black peppercorns

SERVES 4

This meal contains 737 calories per serving, with 23 percent of calories from fat.

Fresh vegetables, wild mushrooms, and a hint of nutmeg flavor this light variation of a traditional French stew. For ease and speed, I have added rice to this recipe so that the entire meal cooks in one frying pan. ¶ Many supermarkets carry several varieties of wild mushrooms. Shiitake mushrooms are available almost year-round, although they are most plentiful in autumn and spring. Their cap is dark brown and they have a meaty flavor. If shiitakes are unavailable, use any other type of wild mushroom, or a mixture of button and wild mushrooms.

FRICASSÉE

3 cups water

1 cup dried lentils

1 tablespoon olive oil

1 medium red onion, sliced (2 cups)

4 medium stalks celery, sliced (2 cups)

2 cups canned, drained sliced red pimientos

6 medium cloves garlic, crushed

2 tablespoons all-purpose flour

1 cup uncooked white basmati rice

1 cup vegetable broth

2 cups dry vermouth

1 ½ pounds shiitake mushrooms, sliced (about 9 cups)

2 tablespoons fresh lemon juice

½ teaspoon ground nutmeg

Salt and freshly ground black pepper to taste

¼ cup chopped fresh parsley

1 French baguette

Preheat oven to 300 degrees F. In a medium-sized saucepan, bring 3 cups water to a boil. Add lentils slowly so that water continues to boil. Cover and simmer 20 minutes. The water will be absorbed and the lentils will be cooked through but will still have a firm texture. Set aside. Meanwhile, heat oil in a nonstick frying pan on medium heat and add onion, celery, pimiento, and garlic. Sauté 1 minute. Sprinkle flour over vegetables and stir until dissolved. Add rice. Combine broth and vermouth and add to frying pan. Bring to a simmer, cover, and let cook gently 10 minutes. Add mushrooms and lentils, replace cover, and simmer 5 minutes. Place bread in oven to warm. Add lemon juice, nutmeg, and salt and pepper to vegetables and mix well. Sprinkle with parsley and serve with warm baguette.

FRENCH BRIE SALAD

8 ounces (4 cups) prewashed mesclun or baby lettuce

4 ounces Brie

¼ cup walnut pieces

2 teaspoons walnut oil

Salt and freshly ground black pepper to taste

Place lettuce on individual plates. Cut cheese in slices 2 x ¼–inch thick (about 12 slices) and place on top of lettuce. Sprinkle with walnuts. Drizzle oil over top. Add salt and pepper to taste.

MODERN
AMERICAN
COMFORT FOODS

HELPFUL HINTS

➤ *Dried mushrooms can be used instead of fresh mushrooms.*

➤ *Any type of lettuce can be used if mesclun or field greens are not available.*

➤ *Any type of soft cheese can be substituted for Brie.*

➤ *Good-quality olive oil can be substituted for walnut oil.*

MUSHROOM STROGANOFF
with BUTTERED EGG NOODLES AND LIMA BEANS

COUNTDOWN

❶ Place water for noodles on to boil.
❷ Start onions for stroganoff.
❸ Prepare remaining ingredients.
❹ Complete stroganoff.
❺ Complete noodles.

SHOPPING LIST

Two 15-ounce cans sliced beets
1 pound mushrooms
1 small bunch fresh parsley
One 8-ounce container
light cream (2⅔ ounces needed)
1 small jar poppy seeds
One 10-ounce package
frozen lima beans

STAPLES

Egg noodles
Red onions (2)
Dijon mustard
Worcestershire sauce
Butter or margarine
Tomato paste
(½ cup needed)
Vegetable broth
(one 14½-ounce can)
All-purpose flour
Salt
Black peppercorns

SERVES 4
This meal contains
786 calories per serving,
with 18 percent
of calories from fat.

The Russian influence on French cuisine was notable long before the Russian Revolution sent the nobility scurrying to Paris for refuge. This stroganoff is a mixture of Russian flavor and French ingenuity. Cooking the onions until they are golden and sweet is the secret. If the onions are undercooked, they will give a raw taste to the meal.

MUSHROOM STROGANOFF

4 teaspoons butter or margarine

2 medium red onions, sliced (4 cups)

1 pound mushrooms, sliced (6 cups)

2 tablespoons all-purpose flour

2 cups vegetable broth

Two 15-ounce cans sliced beets, drained
   (3⅓ cups)

½ cup tomato paste

3 tablespoons Dijon mustard

1 teaspoon Worcestershire sauce

Salt and freshly ground black pepper to taste

⅓ cup light cream

3 tablespoons chopped fresh parsley,
   for garnish (optional)

Heat butter in a medium-sized nonstick frying pan on medium heat. Add onions and sauté until transparent, 10 minutes. If the pan seems very dry, add about ¼ cup of water. Add mushrooms and sauté 1 minute. Stir in flour and sauté 1 minute, making sure flour is absorbed by mushrooms. Pour in broth and mix well. Cut beets into julienne slices (about 2 x ½ inch). Add beets, tomato paste, mustard, Worcestershire, and salt and pepper to taste. You may want to add a little more Worcestershire or mustard, but there should be a delicate blend of flavors with no single flavor dominating. Cook 2 minutes. Remove from heat, stir in cream, and add more salt and pepper, if desired. Serve over the Buttered Egg Noodles and sprinkle parsley on top.

BUTTERED EGG NOODLES AND LIMA BEANS

½ pound uncooked egg noodles

2 tablespoons butter or margarine

2 cups frozen baby lima beans

2 tablespoons poppy seeds

Salt and freshly ground black pepper to taste

Bring a large pot with 3 quarts of water to a boil. Add noodles. Boil about 5 minutes, or according to package instructions. Drain noodles in a colander. While noodles boil, melt butter in a small nonstick frying pan on medium heat. Add lima beans and sauté 2 minutes. Remove pan from heat, add noodles, and toss. Add poppy seeds and salt and pepper to taste. Spoon onto plates and serve with Mushroom Stroganoff on top.

MODERN
AMERICAN
COMFORT FOODS

HELPFUL HINT

➤ *Buy canned beets packed in water, not pickled beets.*

STANLEY'S CASSEROLE SOUP
with CARAMELIZED SHALLOT AND GARLIC TOAST

COUNTDOWN

❶ Start soup.
❷ Start shallots.
❸ Preheat broiler.
❹ Finish soup.
❺ Toast shallot bread.

SHOPPING LIST

I small white cabbage

I pound red potatoes

½ pound shallots

One 10-ounce package prewashed fresh spinach (5 ounces needed)

One 4-ounce package shredded Swiss cheese

Three 14½-ounce cans whole tomatoes (36 ounces needed)

One 16-ounce box fusilli (4 ounces needed)

I loaf country-style bread

STAPLES

Carrots

Celery

Garlic

Red onion

Horseradish

Vegetable broth (two 14½-ounce cans)

Olive oil

Balsamic vinegar

Sugar

Salt

Black peppercorns

SERVES 4

This meal contains 620 calories per serving, with 22 percent of calories from fat.

The warm smell of fresh soup cooking greets me nearly every Saturday morning when I return from walking with my friend Joy, whose husband, Stanley, makes this thick, hearty soup. It is a whole meal in one bowl. This is a shortened version for a midweek dinner. I use shallots for the toast, because they melt away to a paste, leaving a mild onion flavor. The secret is to cook them until they are sweet.

STANLEY'S CASSEROLE SOUP

4 cups vegetable broth

4½ cups canned whole tomatoes, including liquid

1 pound red potatoes, washed and sliced

1 medium red onion, sliced (2 cups)

2 medium carrots, sliced (1 cup)

4 medium celery stalks, sliced (2 cups)

2 cups sliced white cabbage

4 ounces (2 cups) uncooked fusilli

2 tablespoons horseradish

2 tablespoons balsamic vinegar

5 ounces (4 cups) prewashed spinach

4 ounces shredded Swiss cheese

Salt and freshly ground black pepper to taste

Bring vegetable broth, tomatoes, and potatoes to a boil in a large pot on medium-high heat. Add onion, carrots, and celery. Cover, lower heat, and cook on a slow boil 15 minutes. Add cabbage and fusilli. Boil, uncovered, 10 minutes. In a small bowl, mix horseradish and vinegar together. Add to soup along with spinach. Boil 2 minutes. The potatoes and pasta will be cooked and the spinach will be just wilted. Add cheese and salt and pepper to taste. Serve in large soup bowls.

CARAMELIZED SHALLOT AND GARLIC TOAST

2 teaspoons olive oil

½ pound shallots, thinly sliced (2 cups)

8 medium cloves garlic, crushed

1 cup water

2 teaspoons sugar

4 thick slices country-style bread

Heat oil in a medium-sized nonstick frying pan over medium heat. Add shallots and garlic and sauté 1 minute. Add water, cover, and sauté 15 minutes, until water is evaporated. Add sugar and sauté 5 minutes more. The shallots will cook to a spreadable consistency. Spread on bread and toast under boiler 1 to 2 minutes.

MODERN
AMERICAN
COMFORT FOODS

HELPFUL HINTS

➤ *Red or white onions can be used instead of shallots. Be sure to cook them until they are golden and sweet.*

➤ *Any type of thick country-style bread can be used.*

➤ *Slice vegetables in a food processor fitted with a thin slicing blade.*

GRILLED PORTOBELLO STEAK SANDWICH *with* GARLIC FRENCH FRIES

COUNTDOWN

❶ Preheat oven to 400 degrees F.
❷ Marinate mushrooms and onions.
❸ Make potatoes.
❹ Finish sandwich while potatoes cook.

SHOPPING LIST

¾ pound whole portobello mushrooms

2 medium Vidalia onions

2 pounds Russet or Idaho potatoes

1 ripe medium tomato (½ pound)

1 loaf brioche, 4 egg buns, or 1 challah

STAPLES

Garlic

Butter or margarine

Olive oil spray

Balsamic vinegar (16 ounces needed)

Salt

Black peppercorns

SERVES 4

This meal contains 611 calories per serving, with 23 percent of calories from fat.

Dining one evening at Jean Pierre Le Jeune's Gourmet Diner in Miami, I had a delicious marinated mushroom and onion appetizer. I decided it would make a great sandwich. Jean Pierre suggested using brioche or other egg bread, such as challah. I found egg buns at the supermarket and created this modern French dish. It's perfect for a summer barbecue or to create the feeling of one in other seasons. ¶ Meaty portobello mushrooms are perfect for this dish. They cook well in a nonstick frying pan or on a stovetop grill. The secret is to char and crisp the mushrooms and onions. Make sure the mushrooms are drained and dry and the frying pan or grill is smoking hot before adding the mushrooms.

GRILLED PORTOBELLO STEAK SANDWICH

¾ pound whole portobello mushrooms

6 medium cloves garlic, crushed

2 cups balsamic vinegar

1½ medium Vidalia onions, sliced (3 cups)

Olive oil spray

8 slices brioche (or 4 egg buns cut in half,
   or 8 slices challah or other egg bread)

4 teaspoons butter or margarine

1 ripe medium tomato, sliced

Salt and freshly ground black pepper to taste

Wash mushrooms and place in a resealable plastic bag or a small bowl. Add garlic, balsamic vinegar, and onions and marinate 10 minutes. Turn bag over and marinate 10 minutes more. Prepare 2 large nonstick frying pans with olive oil spray and heat on high until smoking. Drain mushrooms, onions, and garlic and discard marinade. Pat mushrooms dry using paper towels and place mushrooms and onions in smoking-hot frying pans. Cook 5 minutes. Turn and cook 3 minutes more. Toast bread and spread with a thin layer of butter. Remove mushrooms to a cutting board and onions to a plate and sprinkle both with salt and pepper to taste. Slice mushrooms ½ inch thick. Place on one slice of bread. Top with onions and sliced tomato. Cover with another slice of bread and serve warm.

GARLIC FRENCH FRIES

Olive oil spray

4 medium Russet or Idaho potatoes
   (2 pounds), scrubbed and sliced into
   4 × ½–inch strips

3 tablespoons melted butter or margarine

4 medium cloves garlic, crushed

Salt and freshly ground black pepper to taste

Preheat broiler. Line a baking tray with aluminum foil and spray with olive oil spray to coat. Melt butter in a microwave-able bowl in microwave oven or in a small saucepan on the stovetop and add crushed garlic. Place potatoes in a bowl or saucepan and toss to coat with butter and garlic. Place potatoes on baking tray and pour any remaining butter and garlic over them. Turn to cover all sides with butter. Place under broiler 5 inches from heat and broil 10 minutes. Remove from broiler, turn potatoes over, and return to broiler to cook 5 minutes more. Add salt and pepper to taste and serve with sandwiches.

MODERN
AMERICAN
COMFORT FOODS

HELPFUL HINTS

➤ *Any sweet onion, such as Texas Sweet or 1040s, can be used. If the very sweet variations are unavailable, use red onions.*

➤ *Crushed garlic is used in both recipes. Crush all at once and use as needed.*

➤ *Use a resealable plastic bag for marinating. It makes for easy clean-up and all you have to do is turn the bag over to make sure the marinade covers all the vegetables.*

➤ *Toast the bread in the oven or under the broiler for a few minutes.*

➤ *If the potatoes don't fit in one layer on a tray, use two trays, placing one below the other on the oven racks. When you remove the top tray to turn the potatoes, move the lower tray to the top to crisp.*

TEX-MEX

SOUTH-
WESTERN

CUISINE

[PICTURED: *Pan-Grilled Quesadillas with Chayote Slaw, page 84*]

GOAT CHEESE ENCHILADAS *with* SWEET CORN SALSA

COUNTDOWN

❶ Preheat oven to 400 degrees F.
❷ Make enchiladas.
❸ While enchiladas cook, make salsa.

SHOPPING LIST

1 large bunch fresh cilantro
1 medium green bell pepper
8 medium jalapeño peppers
2 ripe medium tomatoes
(1 pound)
8 ounces herbed goat cheese
One 4-ounce package
shredded Monterey jack cheese
(1 ounce needed)
Two 19-ounce cans
red kidney beans
Two 28-ounce cans crushed
tomatoes (54 ounces needed)
1 package 8-inch flour tortillas
(6 needed)
One 16-ounce package
frozen corn
(10 ounces needed)

STAPLES

Garlic
Red onion
Distilled white vinegar
Ground coriander
Ground cumin
Sugar
Salt
Black peppercorns

SERVES 4
This meal contains
725 calories per serving,
with 23 percent
of calories from fat.

ortillas made from flour or cornmeal are easy to use, healthy, and readily available. Filled with tangy goat cheese and fresh cilantro and covered with a spicy tomato sauce, these enchiladas are flavorful and fun. Corn salsa completes the earthy Southwestern dinner. ¶ Cooking the tomato sauce with whole jalapeño peppers gives the sauce just a hint of hot spice. If you have a passion for hot peppers, cut the peppers and leave them in the sauce when it is served. ¶ A secret to the enchiladas is to prepare them the Mexican way: Moisten and warm them by dipping in the tomato sauce before filling and rolling.

GOAT CHEESE ENCHILADAS

SAUCE

6 cups canned crushed tomatoes

½ medium red onion, chopped (1 cup)

6 medium jalapeño peppers

Salt and freshly ground black pepper to taste

FILLING

½ pound herbed goat cheese

2 tablespoons ground cumin

3 tablespoons ground coriander

4 medium cloves garlic, crushed

½ cup chopped fresh cilantro

Two 19-ounce cans red kidney beans, drained
and rinsed (4 cups)

1 medium green bell pepper, sliced (1 cup)

2 to 3 tablespoons skim milk (optional)

Six 8-inch flour tortillas

¼ cup shredded Monterey jack cheese,
for garnish

¼ cup chopped red onion, for garnish

Preheat oven to 400 degrees F. Line a baking tray with aluminum foil.

To make the sauce, place crushed tomatoes, 1 cup onion, and whole jalapeño peppers in a large saucepan and bring to a boil. Reduce heat and simmer, uncovered 10 minutes. Remove from heat and add salt and pepper to taste.

To make the filling, mix goat cheese, cumin, coriander, garlic, cilantro, and green bell pepper together. (If using a food processor, chop green bell pepper, then add cilantro, spices, and goat cheese.) Add beans and combine. If the mixture seems stiff and dry, add skim milk to moisten and soften. Divide into 6 portions.

To fill enchiladas, dip tortillas in tomato sauce. Make sure they are completely covered in sauce. Remove to baking tray and spoon one portion of filling into the center of each tortilla. Roll up and place seam side down on tray. Spoon half the sauce over enchiladas and cover with aluminum foil. Place in oven 10 minutes while you make the salsa. To serve, remove jalapeño peppers from pan. Place 1½ enchiladas on each plate and spoon remaining sauce over top. Sprinkle with cheese and onion. Serve with Sweet Corn Salsa.

 SWEET CORN SALSA
recipe follows

HELPFUL HINTS

➤ *Other cheeses, such as Cheddar or Fontina, may be used if Monterey jack is unavailable. Use prepackaged shredded cheese, if available.*

➤ *If pressed for time, use a bottled or canned tomato sauce and warm it with the hot peppers, and buy a chunky salsa instead of making the corn salsa.*

➤ *To wash the cilantro quickly, immerse it in a bowl of water for several minutes while you prepare the other ingredients. Lift it out of the water, shake it dry, and it's ready to use.*

➤ *Onion and cilantro are used in both recipes. Coarsely chop all of the onion (1¾ cups) at once, remove, and use as needed. Chop the cilantro (1 cup) at once, remove and use as needed.*

➤ *To save time, make the filling in the food processor.*

SWEET CORN SALSA

2 cups frozen or drained canned corn

2 ripe medium tomatoes, diced (2 cups)

½ cup chopped fresh cilantro

¼ medium red onion, chopped (½ cup)

2 medium jalapeño peppers, seeded and chopped

½ teaspoon sugar

1 teaspoon ground cumin

2 tablespoons distilled white vinegar

Salt and freshly ground black pepper to taste

If using frozen corn, defrost for 2 minutes in a microwave on "high." In a large bowl, combine corn and tomatoes. Add cilantro, onion, peppers, sugar, and cumin and gently toss. Add vinegar and salt and pepper to taste. Toss again and serve.

TEX-MEX
AND
SOUTH-WESTERN
CUISINE

PICTURED:

Goat Cheese Enchiladas with Sweet Corn Salsa

SKILLET PASTA PIE
with BLACK BEAN SALAD

C
O
U
N
T
D
O
W
N

❶ Place water for pasta on to boil.
❷ Make pasta.
❸ Make salad.

SHOPPING LIST

1 small bunch fresh cilantro

1 lime (if making dressing)

One 10-ounce package prewashed lettuce (8 ounces needed)

½ pound mushrooms

1 medium green bell pepper

One 8-ounce package hot pepper Monterey jack cheese (4 ounces needed)

One 16-ounce can black beans

Two 28-ounce cans crushed tomatoes (36 ounces needed)

½ pound fresh fettuccini or one 16-ounce package dried fettuccini (8 ounces needed)

1 small package dried chipotle peppers

One 16-ounce package frozen corn (10 ounces needed)

STAPLES

Garlic

Yellow onion

Low-fat or fat-free salad dressing, or Dijon mustard and olive oil

Olive oil spray

Ground cumin

Salt

Black peppercorns

SERVES 4
This meal contains 627 calories per serving, with 24 percent of calories from fat.

The pasta and sauce for this pasta-based pie cook together in a frying pan, so the pasta absorbs the sauce flavors. Just bring the frying pan to the table and cut and serve wedges, like a pie. Serve the pie on its own or, if you have time, make this quick black bean salad to serve with it.

SKILLET PASTA PIE

¼ cup water

Olive oil spray

3 small chipotle peppers

1 medium yellow onion, sliced (2 cups)

5 medium cloves garlic, crushed

1 medium green bell pepper, sliced (1 cup)

½ pound mushrooms, sliced (3 cups)

4 cups canned crushed tomatoes

2 teaspoons ground cumin

2 cups frozen corn

Salt and freshly ground black pepper to taste

½ pound uncooked fresh or dried fettuccini

⅔ cup hot pepper Monterey jack cheese, grated

½ cup chopped fresh cilantro, for garnish

Place a large pot filled with 3 to 4 quarts water on to boil. Heat ¼ cup water in a microwave oven or on the stovetop in a small saucepan and soak chipotle peppers in the warm water 10 minutes. Prepare a 10-inch nonstick frying pan along with olive oil spray and place on burner over medium heat. Add onion, garlic, green bell pepper, and mushrooms. Sauté 10 minutes. Remove chipotle peppers from water and chop. Add to frying pan with tomato, cumin, corn, and salt and pepper to taste and simmer gently 5 minutes.

Meanwhile, place fettuccini in boiling water and cook 2 to 3 minutes if using fresh pasta, 9 minutes if using dried. Drain pasta in a colander and add to skillet. Cook 10 minutes more, blending the sauce and noodles together as they cook. Make sure pasta and sauce are well blended. Remove from heat and sprinkle cheese on top. Cover and remove from heat to let cheese melt, 3 minutes. Sprinkle cilantro on top. Cut into wedges and serve.

 BLACK BEAN SALAD
recipe follows

HELPFUL HINTS

➤ *Cheddar or Fontina cheeses may be used if hot pepper Monterey jack is unavailable.*

➤ *Use dried fettuccini or tagliatelli if fresh fettuccini is unavailable.*

➤ *Any type of prewashed salad can be used.*

➤ *Slice the vegetables in a food processor. Onions, green bell pepper, and mushrooms can be prepared in sequence without emptying the bowl.*

BLACK BEAN SALAD

2 cups canned black beans, drained and rinsed

¼ cup low-fat or fat-free dressing, or
   2 tablespoons fresh lime juice,
   2 teaspoons Dijon mustard, ¼ cup water,
   and 4 teaspoons olive oil

Salt and freshly ground black pepper to taste

8 ounces (4 cups) prewashed lettuce

In a salad bowl, toss black beans with
bottled dressing or mix lime juice, mustard,
water, and oil together in the bowl and toss
with beans. Add salt and pepper to taste.
Place lettuce in bowl and toss with beans.

TEX-MEX

AND

SOUTH-WESTERN

CUISINE

PICTURED:

*Skillet Pasta Pie with
Black Bean Salad*

SOUTHWESTERN THREE-BEAN SOUP
with CUCUMBER AND JICAMA SALAD

C O U N T D O W N

❶ Preheat oven to 350 degrees F to warm bread.
❷ Make soup.
❸ While soup cooks, make salad.

SHOPPING LIST

1 small bunch fresh cilantro
1 medium cucumber
½ pound jicama
1 lime (if making dressing)
1 medium parsnip
1 medium jalapeño pepper
One 19-ounce can chickpeas
One 19-ounce can red kidney beans
Two 28-ounce cans whole tomatoes
1 French baguette
One 10-ounce package frozen baby lima beans

STAPLES

Carrots
Red onion
Low-fat or fat-free salad dressing
Olive oil
Chili powder
Ground cumin
Salt
Black peppercorns

SERVES 4

This meal contains 775 calories per serving, with 17 percent of calories from fat.

T hick, hearty soup and a refreshing salad make a great twenty-five-minute winter dinner. The soup is a flavor-packed meal in a bowl. It freezes well. If you have time, double the recipe and you will have another meal ready in minutes. ¶ Jicama is a root vegetable with a thin brown skin and slightly sweet crunchy white flesh, found in most supermarkets. It should be peeled just before use. The nutty flavor and crisp texture provide a refreshing contrast to the thick soup.

SOUTHWESTERN THREE-BEAN SOUP

4 ½ cups water, divided

1 medium red onion, sliced (2 cups)

2 medium carrots, sliced (1 cup)

1 medium parsnip, sliced (1 cup)

One 19-ounce can red kidney beans, drained and rinsed (2 cups)

One 10-ounce package frozen baby lima beans (2 cups)

One 19-ounce can chickpeas, drained and rinsed (2 cups)

Two 28-ounce cans whole tomatoes (7 cups)

2 teaspoons ground cumin

4 teaspoons chili powder

2 tablespoons olive oil

Salt and freshly ground black pepper to taste

¼ cup chopped fresh cilantro

1 French baguette

Preheat oven to 350 degrees F. Place a large saucepan on medium heat and add ½ cup water. Add onion, carrots, and parsnip and sauté 5 minutes. Add all beans, chickpeas, tomatoes, the remaining 4 cups water, cumin, and chili powder. Break up tomatoes with a spoon or knife and bring to a simmer. Simmer 20 minutes. Stir in the olive oil and add salt and pepper to taste. Place bread in oven to warm for 5 minutes. Ladle soup into bowls, sprinkle with cilantro and serve with warm bread.

CUCUMBER AND JICAMA SALAD

4 tablespoons low-fat or fat-free salad dressing, or 2 tablespoons fresh lime juice, 2 teaspoons olive oil, and 4 tablespoons water

2 tablespoons sliced red onion

1 medium jalapeño pepper, seeded and chopped

1 medium cucumber, peeled, cut in half lengthwise, and sliced into ½-inch pieces (2 cups)

½ pound jicama, peeled, and sliced into ½-inch pieces (2 cups)

Salt and freshly ground black pepper to taste

Pour bottled salad dressing into a salad bowl or whisk lime juice, olive oil, and water together in the bowl. Add onion, jalapeño pepper, cucumber, and jicama and toss. Add salt and pepper to taste.

TEX-MEX
AND
SOUTH-WESTERN
CUISINE

HELPFUL HINTS

➤ *If you can't find jicama, use any crunchy vegetable, such as celery, instead.*

➤ *Onion is used in both recipes. Prepare all at once and use as needed.*

MEXICAN CHILI
with TORTILLA SALAD

C O U N T D O W N

❶ Preheat oven to 350 degrees F.
❷ Make chili.
❸ While chili cooks, make salad.

SHOPPING LIST

1 large bunch fresh cilantro

1 medium green bell pepper

4 medium jalapeño peppers

One 10-ounce package prewashed lettuce, primarily romaine (8 ounces needed)

2 ripe medium tomatoes (1 pound)

One 8-ounce container low-fat sour cream (2 ounces needed)

Two 16-ounce cans red kidney beans

One 15½-ounce can hominy (5 ounces needed)

Two 28-ounce cans crushed tomatoes (36 ounces needed)

1 package low-fat tortilla chips

1 loaf crusty sourdough bread

One 32-ounce package frozen corn (20 to 25 ounces needed)

STAPLES

Carrots

Celery

Garlic

Lemons (2)

Red onion

Canola oil

Olive oil

Olive oil spray

Chili powder

Ground cumin

Salt

Black peppercorns

SERVES 4

This meal contains 792 calories per serving, with 11 percent of calories from fat.

his chili takes only thirty minutes to make but tastes like it simmered all day. Hominy is a dried white or yellow corn that has been soaked or boiled to remove the hulls. Sold canned or dried, it gives the chili an interesting texture. This dinner freezes well; make extra and you'll have another quick dinner ready.

82

MEXICAN CHILI

2 teaspoons olive oil

1 medium red onion, sliced (2 cups)

4 medium cloves garlic, crushed

2 medium stalks celery, sliced (½ cup)

1 medium green bell pepper, sliced (1 cup)

4 medium carrots, diced (1 cup)

Two 16-ounce cans red kidney beans, drained
and rinsed (3 cups)

36 ounces canned crushed tomatoes (4 cups)

1 cup drained and rinsed canned hominy
or 1 cup frozen corn

3 tablespoons chili powder

2 teaspoons ground cumin

Salt and freshly ground black pepper to taste

1 loaf crusty sourdough bread

¼ cup low-fat sour cream, for garnish

¼ cup sliced red onion, for garnish

1 cup chopped fresh cilantro, for garnish

Preheat oven to 350 degrees F. Heat oil in a
large nonstick saucepan on medium heat.
Add onion and sauté 3 minutes. Add garlic,
celery, green bell pepper, and carrots and
sauté 5 minutes. Add kidney beans, tomatoes, hominy, chili powder, and cumin.
Simmer 20 minutes. Add salt and pepper to
taste. Add more chili powder or cumin as
desired. Warm bread in oven 5 minutes.
Slice and serve with chili. Serve chili,
passing bowls of sour cream, onion, and
cilantro to sprinkle on top.

MEXICAN TORTILLA SALAD

4 cups frozen or drained canned corn

8 ounces prewashed lettuce, primarily romaine
(4 cups)

1 ripe medium tomato, diced
(about 1½ cups)

½ cup chopped fresh cilantro

2 tablespoons fresh lemon juice

4 tablespoons water

1 tablespoon canola oil

2 medium jalapeño peppers, chopped
(2 tablespoons)

2 medium cloves garlic, crushed

2 teaspoons ground cumin

Salt and freshly ground black pepper to taste

2 cups low-fat tortilla chips

If using frozen corn, warm in microwave
oven 2 minutes on "high," or boil in a little
water for 2 minutes and drain. If using
canned corn, drain well. Place lettuce in a
salad bowl with tomato, corn, and cilantro.
To make the dressing, whisk lemon juice,
water, and oil together. Add jalapeño
peppers, garlic, and cumin. Add salt and
pepper to taste. Pour dressing over salad
and toss well. Top with tortilla chips.

TEX-MEX
AND
SOUTH-
WESTERN
CUISINE

HELPFUL HINTS

➤ *If pressed for time, use
a bottled low-fat salad
dressing.*

➤ *Frozen or canned corn
can be used if hominy is
unavailable.*

➤ *Slice the vegetables in a
food processor.*

➤ *Red onion is used both for
the garnish and recipe.
Prepare it all at once and
reserve 2 tablespoons for
the garnish.*

➤ *For fluffy rice, boil rice as
you would pasta, in a pot
large enough to let the
grains roll freely in the
boiling water.*

PAN-GRILLED QUESADILLAS *with* CHAYOTE SLAW

C O U N T D O W N

❶ Prepare chayote slaw.
❷ Prepare quesadilla.

SHOPPING LIST

1 medium chayote
1 small bunch fresh cilantro
1 small jicama
3 medium jalapeño peppers
One 4-ounce package
shredded Monterey jack cheese
One 19-ounce can white beans
(navy or cannellini)
Two 7½-ounce cans
sliced red pimientos
1 package 8-inch flour tortillas
(12 needed)

STAPLES

Carrots
Garlic
Red onion
Dijon mustard
Hot pepper sauce
Honey
Low-fat mayonnaise
Distilled white vinegar
Sugar
Salt
Black peppercorns

SERVES 4
This meal contains
561 calories per serving,
with 26 percent
of calories from fat.

Pan-grilled flour tortillas filled with a savory bean mixture and melted Monterey jack cheese make a quick Southwestern dinner. Quesadillas can be served as an appetizer or a full meal. Once filled and sandwiched together they only take two minutes each to cook or six minutes for all six when using two frying pans. ¶ Jicama is a root vegetable with a thin brown skin and white crunchy flesh similar in texture to a water chestnut. Served raw or cooked, it retains its crisp water-chestnut texture. If difficult to find, substitute green cabbage in the slaw. Chayote, or christophene, tastes like a cross between cucumber and zucchini, with a slightly crisp texture when served raw. When steamed it tastes more like zucchini. It is low in calories and a good source of fiber and potassium.

PAN-GRILLED QUESADILLAS

6 medium cloves garlic

¼ cup sliced red onion

Two 7½-ounce cans sliced red pimientos, drained (1 cup)

One 19-ounce can white beans (navy or cannellini), drained and rinsed (2 cups)

Several drops hot pepper sauce

Salt and freshly ground black pepper to taste

Twelve 8-inch flour tortillas

1 cup shredded Monterey jack cheese

3 medium jalapeño peppers, seeded and chopped

½ cup chopped fresh cilantro

Using a food processor fitted with the chopping blade, pulse briefly to chop garlic, onion, and pimiento. Add beans and hot pepper sauce and purée. If mixing by hand, mash beans with a fork, chop pimiento, crush garlic, dice onion, and mix together, adding hot pepper sauce. Add salt and pepper to taste. Spread 6 tortillas with bean mixture. Sprinkle cheese, jalapeño peppers, and cilantro on top. Cover each with 1 of the 6 remaining tortillas. To cook, heat two large nonstick frying pans on high heat. When hot, place 1 quesadilla in each pan. Heat 1 minute, turn over, heat 1 minute more, and remove to a cutting board. Continue until all 6 quesadillas are cooked. Cut each quesadilla into 4 wedges. Place 6 wedges on each plate and serve with jicama slaw.

CHAYOTE SLAW

¼ cup low-fat mayonnaise

2 tablespoons distilled white vinegar

2 tablespoons Dijon mustard

1 tablespoon honey

1 whole chayote, grated (2 cups)

1 jicama, peeled and grated (1 cup)

½ medium red onion, grated or cut into julienne slices (1 cup)

2 medium carrots, grated or cut into julienne slices (1 cup)

Salt and freshly ground black pepper to taste

2 tablespoons chopped fresh cilantro, for garnish

Whisk mayonnaise, vinegar, mustard, and honey together in a small salad bowl. Add vegetables and salt and pepper to taste. Toss well. Let vegetables marinate while you prepare quesadilla. Top with cilantro and serve.

TEX-MEX
AND
SOUTH-WESTERN
CUISINE

HELPFUL HINTS

➤ *Red onion is used in both recipes. Chop all at once and use as needed.*

➤ *For Chayote Slaw, chayote, jicama, onion, and carrots may be prepared in a food processor fitted with grating blade or slicing blade.*

CHILES EN NOGADA
(STUFFED CHILES IN WALNUT SAUCE)
with PIMIENTO RICE

C O U N T D O W N

❶ Preheat broiler.
❷ Start rice.
❸ While rice boils, broil peppers.
❹ Prepare stuffing.
❺ Finish rice.
❻ Complete stuffed peppers.

SHOPPING LIST

2 large green bell peppers or
4 small poblanos

4 medium jalapeño peppers

One 8-ounce container low-fat
sour cream (4 ounces needed)

One 19-ounce can
red kidney beans

One 28-ounce can crushed
tomatoes (19 ounces needed)

One 7½-ounce can
whole red pimientos

One 2½-ounce package
walnut pieces (1 ounce needed)

STAPLES

Garlic

Red onion

Skim milk

Raisins

Long-grain white rice

Olive oil

Ground cinnamon

Ground cumin

Sugar

Salt

Black peppercorns

SERVES 4
This meal contains
546 calories per serving,
with 23 percent
of calories from fat.

his enticing dish—stuffed green bell peppers, white walnut sauce, and red pimientos—is often called Mexico's national dish. The green, white, and red are the colors of the Mexican flag. Nogada, a white sauce delicately flavored with walnuts, is served cold over the warm stuffed peppers. The peppers are traditionally stuffed with picadillo, a dish made with ground pork, beef, or veal, tomatoes, garlic, onions, raisins, and, sometimes, capers. For this recipe, red beans replace the meat, with a light, tasty result. ¶ Poblano peppers, a dark green, mildly hot chile pepper, are sold fresh in some supermarkets. I use green bell peppers because they are easier to find. The peppers are slightly charred under the broiler for a few minutes, then stuffed. Charred peppers are usually peeled, but with the filling and sauce, the skin isn't noticed and actually adds a lot of flavor. ¶ Although the recipe looks complicated, it takes only 45 minutes to make and is worth the effort.

CHILES EN NOGADA (STUFFED CHILES IN WALNUT SAUCE)

2 large green bell peppers, or 4 small poblanos

SAUCE

¼ cup chopped walnuts

½ cup low-fat sour cream

¼ cup skim milk

1 teaspoon ground cinnamon

4 teaspoons sugar

STUFFING

½ cup chopped red onion

4 medium jalapeño peppers, washed and seeded

2 medium cloves garlic

2 cups canned red kidney beans, drained and rinsed

4 teaspoons ground cumin

2 teaspoons olive oil

2 cups canned crushed tomatoes

¼ cup raisins

Preheat broiler. Place green bell peppers on aluminum foil–lined baking tray. Broil 2 inches from heat 5 minutes. Turn and broil 5 minutes more. Be careful not to over-cook. Remove peppers from broiler and turn off heat.

Meanwhile, to make the sauce, chop walnuts in the food processor. In a small bowl, mix sour cream and skim milk together until smooth. Add walnuts, cinnamon, and sugar and stir to blend.

To make the stuffing, chop onion in food processor. With machine running, add jalapeño peppers and garlic. Stop processor, add red beans and cumin, and process until coarsely chopped. Heat olive oil in a medium-sized nonstick frying pan on medium-high heat, add bean mixture, and sauté 1 minute. Add tomatoes and raisins and sauté 2 minutes. Remove from heat and set aside.

When ready to serve, cut peppers in half and remove seeds. Return to tray and fill each half with bean mixture. Place tray in warm oven until needed. (The heat from the broiler will keep peppers warm.) Remove peppers from oven. Place on individual plates, spoon sauce over top, and serve.

 PIMIENTO RICE
recipe follows

HELPFUL HINTS

➤ *Heat broiler before you start to gather ingredients. It must be hot to char the peppers.*

➤ *For fluffy rice, boil rice as you would pasta, in a pot large enough to let the grains roll freely in the boiling water.*

➤ *To avoid having to wash the bowl of the food processor when chopping the ingredients, chop the walnuts first, remove, then chop the stuffing ingredients.*

PIMIENTO RICE

1 cup uncooked long-grain white rice
One 7½-ounce can whole red pimientos,
  drained and diced (½ cup)
4 teaspoons olive oil
Salt and freshly ground black pepper to taste

Bring a large pot filled with 2 to 3 quarts of
water to a boil. Add rice and boil, uncovered, about 10 minutes. Test a grain. Rice
should be cooked through, but not soft.
Drain in a colander. Place in a serving bowl
and add pimiento and olive oil. Toss well.
Add salt and pepper, to taste.

TEX-MEX
AND
SOUTH-
WESTERN
CUISINE

PICTURED:

*Chiles en Nogada with
Pimiento Rice*

FAJITAS *with* REFRIED BEANS

C O U N T D O W N

❶ Prepare vegetables for fajitas and refried beans.

❷ Marinate mushrooms.

❸ While mushrooms marinate, make refried beans.

❹ While beans cook, make fajitas.

SHOPPING LIST

1 medium bunch fresh cilantro

½ pound portobello mushrooms

1 medium green bell pepper

1 medium red bell pepper

3 medium jalapeño peppers

3 ripe medium tomatoes (1½ pounds)

One 4-ounce package shredded Monterey jack or Cheddar cheese (2 ounces needed)

One 8-ounce container nonfat sour cream (4 ounces needed)

Two 16-ounce cans pinto beans (19 ounces needed)

One package 8-inch flour tortillas (8 needed)

STAPLES

Garlic

Lemon

Red onions (2)

Vegetable broth (one 14½-ounce can)

Canola oil

Olive oil spray

Cayenne pepper

Ground cumin

Salt

SERVES 4

This meal contains 690 calories per serving, with 23 percent of calories from fat.

Southwestern fajitas make a delicious light meal. Served with an array of colorful vegetables to wrap in warm tortillas, they're fun to eat, as everyone helps themselves to their favorite fillers. These little Mexican sandwiches are an entire meal in themselves and can be served on their own, or make these quick refried beans to serve with them.

FAJITAS

½ cup fresh lemon juice

2 tablespoons canola oil

2 teaspoons ground cumin

½ teaspoon cayenne pepper

Eight 8-inch flour tortillas

½ pound portobello mushrooms, sliced
   (about 5 cups)

Olive oil spray

1 medium red onion, sliced (2 cups)

½ medium red bell pepper, sliced (½ cup)

½ medium green bell pepper, sliced (½ cup)

4 medium cloves garlic, crushed

2 ripe medium tomatoes, diced (2 cups)

½ cup chopped fresh cilantro

½ cup grated Monterey jack or
   Cheddar cheese

½ cup nonfat sour cream

Mix lemon juice, canola oil, cumin, and cayenne together in a microwaveable bowl. Heat for 1 minute in microwave oven on "high," or mix ingredients in a saucepan and bring to a boil. Remove from heat. Add mushrooms to marinade, stirring to cover mushrooms completely. Place mushrooms and marinade in a large resealable plastic bag, close, and let marinate for 15 minutes, turning once while marinating.

Drain mushrooms, reserving marinade. Tightly wrap 4 of the tortillas in a paper towel and the remaining 4 in a second paper towel. Place both packages in the microwave oven and heat on "high" 1 minute. Remove and leave wrapped.

Prepare a large nonstick frying pan with olive oil spray and heat on high heat until smoking. Add drained mushrooms and sauté on high heat 30 seconds. Add onion, bell peppers, and garlic and sauté 3 minutes. Add remaining marinade and toss 1 minute.

To serve, mix tomatoes and cilantro together, add salt and pepper to taste, and place in a small serving bowl. Place the grated cheese and sour cream in separate small bowls. Spoon the vegetables onto a warm serving dish and place the tortillas in another dish, covered by a cloth napkin or a piece of aluminum foil to keep warm. Each person can fill a tortilla with some or all of the ingredients. Once ingredients have been selected, roll up tortilla and eat like a sandwich.

 REFRIED BEANS
recipe follows

HELPFUL HINTS

➤ *Use a food processor fitted with the slicing blade for thick-sliced vegetables, then change blades to coarsely chop vegetables for the refried beans.*

➤ *Cut vegetables for both recipes at once and place in small bowls or in piles on a cutting board.*

➤ *Use a resealable plastic bag for marinating. To turn mushrooms over, simply flip the bag over.*

REFRIED BEANS

1 cup vegetable broth, divided

½ medium red onion, sliced (1 cup)

1 medium clove garlic, crushed

2 tablespoons chopped fresh cilantro

1 ripe medium tomato, diced (1 cup)

3 medium jalapeño peppers, seeded and chopped

2 cups canned pinto beans, drained and rinsed

2 teaspoons canola oil

Salt to taste

Heat 2 tablespoons of the vegetable broth in a medium-sized nonstick frying pan on medium heat. Add onion and garlic and sauté 5 minutes. Set aside. In a food processor fitted with the chopping blade, coarsely chop cilantro, tomato, jalapeño peppers, and beans. Or, chop cilantro, tomato, jalapeño peppers, and beans by hand. Set aside. Add oil to remaining vegetable broth. Add ¼ cup of the oil-broth mixture to frying pan containing onions and garlic and add bean mixture. Mix well. Sauté on medium-high heat 5 minutes, stirring frequently. Make a depression in center of beans and add remaining broth. Cook 5 minutes, occasionally scraping the sides of the pan. For firmer refried beans, cook 5 minutes more. Add salt to taste. Serve with fajitas.

TEX-MEX
AND
SOUTH-
WESTERN
CUISINE

PICTURED:

Fajitas with Refried Beans

BLACK BEAN CHILI
with MEXICAN WHITE RICE

COUNTDOWN

❶ Preheat oven to 350 degrees F.
❷ Make chili.
❸ While chili cooks, make rice.

SHOPPING LIST

¾ pound broccoli florets

1 small bunch fresh cilantro

1 medium red bell pepper

4 medium jalapeño peppers

1 small bunch scallions

2 ripe medium tomatoes
(1 pound)

One 4-ounce package
shredded Monterey jack cheese
(1 ounce needed)

Two 16-ounce cans black beans

1 small loaf crusty
sourdough bread

One 16-ounce package
frozen corn (10 ounces needed)

STAPLES

Garlic

Red onions (2)

Tomato paste

Vegetable broth
(two 14½-ounce cans)

Long-grain white rice

Olive oil

Olive oil spray

Chili powder

Ground cumin

Salt

Black peppercorns

SERVES 4

This meal contains
786 calories per serving,
with 15 percent
of calories from fat.

This quick black bean chili is great for a weeknight meal or perfect for a casual party. It's an easy recipe to double or triple as needed. You can make the chili in advance and freeze it, or make it a day ahead and refrigerate it. ¶ For a casual dinner with friends, leave the pot of chili on the stove and let everyone help themselves. A basket of warm bread and a salad made with packaged prewashed lettuce complete this quick dinner. If you're pressed for time, use a packaged quick-cooking rice instead of the Mexican White Rice.

BLACK BEAN CHILI

2 teaspoons olive oil

1 medium red onion, sliced (2 cups)

4 medium cloves garlic, crushed

1 medium red bell pepper, sliced (1 cup)

Two 16-ounce cans black beans, drained and rinsed (3 cups)

2 ripe medium tomatoes, cut into 2-inch pieces (2 cups)

2 cups frozen or drained canned corn

3 tablespoons chili powder

2 teaspoons ground cumin

2 tablespoons tomato paste

2 cups vegetable broth

2 cups broccoli florets (cut in half if large)

Salt and freshly ground black pepper to taste

1 loaf crusty sourdough bread

¼ cup shredded Monterey Jack cheese, for garnish

4 scallions, sliced (1 cup), for garnish

Preheat oven to 350 degrees F. Heat oil in a large nonstick frying pan on medium-high heat. Add onion and sauté 3 minutes. Add garlic and red bell pepper and sauté 3 minutes. Add black beans, tomatoes, corn, chili powder, and cumin. In a bowl, mix tomato paste into broth, then stir into chili. Simmer, covered, 10 minutes. Add broccoli and simmer, covered, 5 minutes more. Add salt and pepper and taste for seasoning. Add more chili powder or cumin as desired. Warm bread in oven 5 minutes. Slice and serve with chili. Serve chili over rice and pass cheese and scallions to sprinkle on top.

MEXICAN WHITE RICE

Olive oil spray

1 medium red onion, sliced (2 cups)

4 medium cloves garlic, crushed

1 cup uncooked long-grain white rice

2 cups vegetable broth

4 whole medium jalapeño peppers

4 teaspoons olive oil

Salt and freshly ground black pepper to taste

1 cup chopped fresh cilantro, for garnish

Prepare a large nonstick frying pan with olive oil spray and heat on medium-high heat. Add onion and garlic and sauté 2 minutes. Do not brown. Add rice and sauté 30 seconds. Add broth, jalapeño peppers, and oil. Cover and simmer 15 minutes. Add salt and pepper to taste. Remove peppers, top with cilantro, and serve.

TEX-MEX
AND
SOUTH-WESTERN
CUISINE

HELPFUL HINTS

➤ *Buy tomato paste in a tube. You can use a small amount and the tube can be stored in the refrigerator until needed again.*

➤ *The vegetables can be sliced in a food processor or diced by hand.*

➤ *Red onion is used in both recipes. Slice all at once and use as needed.*

FOODS OF THE

FAR EAST

VEGETABLE LO MEIN
with CHINESE SALAD

C O U N T D O W N

❶ Place water for noodles on to boil.
❷ Prepare sauce.
❸ Wash and cut vegetables.
❹ Cook noodles.
❺ Stir-fry vegetables and noodles.
❻ Make salad.

SHOPPING LIST

½ pound fresh bean sprouts
1 medium cucumber
2-inch piece gingerroot
1 small head iceberg lettuce
½ pound mushrooms
½ pound fresh snow peas
¾ pound fresh or dried
Chinese steamed egg noodles

STAPLES

Carrots
Celery
Garlic
Yellow onions (2)
Low-salt soy sauce
Dijon mustard
Honey
Cornstarch
Sesame oil
Oriental rice wine vinegar
Dry sherry
Cayenne pepper

SERVES 4
This meal contains
700 calories per serving,
with 25 percent
of calories from fat.

Fresh noodles are a staple of the northern Chinese diet in areas where it is too cold to grow rice. Homemade noodles are served on birthdays as a symbol of long life. Lo mein is a traditional stir-fry of soft noodles, vegetables, and meat. Most supermarkets sell fresh Chinese steamed egg noodles in the refrigerated section of the produce department. Dried Chinese steamed egg noodles can be found in the ethnic foods section of supermarkets. Either type works fine in this recipe. If Chinese noodles are difficult to find, use spaghettini or angel hair pasta. The vegetables in this dish were selected for their varied flavors, colors, and textures.

VEGETABLE LO MEIN

¾ pound uncooked fresh or dried Chinese
   steamed egg noodles
¼ cup low-salt soy sauce
¼ cup dry sherry
2 tablespoons chopped gingerroot
6 medium cloves garlic, crushed
¼ cup cornstarch
½ teaspoon cayenne pepper
4 tablespoons sesame oil, divided
1½ medium yellow onions, sliced (3 cups)
4 medium carrots, sliced (2 cups)
4 medium celery stalks, sliced (2 cups)
½ pound fresh snow peas (3 cups)
½ pound fresh bean sprouts (3 cups)
½ pound mushrooms (3 cups)
Low-salt soy sauce

Fill a large pot half-full with water, bring
to a boil, and add noodles. Boil 2 to 3 minutes and drain in a colander. To prepare
sauce and vegetables, in a large bowl mix
the soy sauce, sherry, ginger, garlic, cornstarch, cayenne pepper, and 1 tablespoon of
the sesame oil together. Heat another 1
tablespoon of the sesame oil in a large wok
or frying pan.

When the pan is very hot, add onions and
stir-fry 1 minute. Add carrots and celery
and cook 2 minutes. Add snow peas, bean
sprouts, and mushrooms and cook 1
minute. Add drained noodles. Stir-fry
2 to 3 minutes, stirring constantly to mix
noodles and vegetables. Add sauce and
continue tossing 2 minutes more. Add
remaining 2 tablespoons sesame oil. Toss
to blend well and serve. Serve with soy
sauce to sprinkle on as desired.

CHINESE SALAD

1 medium cucumber, peeled and cut into
   2 x ¼-inch strips (2 cups)
½ small head iceberg lettuce, cut into
   ¼-inch-wide strips (4 cups)
¼ cup Oriental rice wine vinegar
2 teaspoons Dijon mustard
2 medium cloves garlic, crushed
4 teaspoons honey
2 teaspoons sesame oil

Layer lettuce and cucumber on a serving
platter or divide between 2 plates. Whisk
vinegar and mustard together in a small
bowl. Add garlic and honey. Blend until
smooth and whisk in oil. Spoon over
cucumber and lettuce.

FOODS OF THE
FAR EAST

HELPFUL HINTS

➤ *Crushed garlic is used in
both recipes. Crush all at
once and use as needed.*

➤ *Use a food processor fitted
with a slicing blade to cut
cucumber and lettuce for
salad.*

➤ *Arrange all of the ingredients on a cutting board or
a plate in order of use.*

➤ *You will need a large
wok or frying pan, or use
2 woks or pans, to give the
vegetables plenty of room.*

➤ *Make sure your wok or
frying pan is very hot
before you start to stir-fry.*

CHINESE STEAMBOAT

C
O
U
N
T
D
O
W
N

❶ Prepare braised tofu.
❷ Start broth.
❸ Prepare remaining ingredients.

SHOPPING LIST

½ pound bok choy
One 2-inch piece gingerroot
½ pound mushrooms
½ pound snow peas
1 small bunch scallions
½ pound fresh or dried
Chinese steamed egg noodles
1 pound firm tofu

STAPLES

Carrots
Yellow onion
Low-salt soy sauce
Vegetable broth
(two 14½-ounce cans)
Sesame oil
Dry sherry
Dark brown sugar

SERVES 4
This meal contains
590 calories per serving,
with 24 percent
of calories from fat.

While visiting Malaysia, I was introduced to this special dish. Chinese Steamboat is very much like a fondue or hot pot. A large pot is placed on a burner in the center of the table and everyone cooks their own food. I have found that everyone loves to participate in the cooking process. ¶ This is a perfect one-pot meal when you're in a hurry, since most of the cooking is done at the table. The vegetables are dipped into the broth to cook and then dipped into a savory sauce. To finish the meal, the hearty broth is poured into soup bowls with the remaining dipping sauce. ¶ You will need either a fondue pot with a burner or a saucepan placed on a portable electric or gas burner. An electric frying pan or wok also works well. If none of these pans is available, you can make a delicious soup variation (page 103).

CHINESE STEAMBOAT

BRAISED TOFU
2 tablespoons low-salt soy sauce

4 teaspoons dark brown sugar

¼ cup water

4 teaspoons sesame oil

1 pound firm tofu, drained and cut in
 1-inch dice

BROTH
Two 14½-ounce cans vegetable broth

3⅓ cups water

4 medium carrots, sliced (2 cups)

1 medium yellow onion, sliced (2 cups)

VEGETABLES
½ pound bok choy (6 cups)

½ pound mushrooms (3 cups)

½ pound fresh snow peas (2 cups)

½ pound uncooked fresh or dried Chinese
 steamed egg noodles (3½ cups)

DIPPING SAUCE
⅓ cup low-salt soy sauce

⅓ cup dry sherry

2 tablespoons dark brown sugar

2 teaspoons sesame oil

6 scallions, sliced (1 cup)

2-inch piece gingerroot, peeled and chopped
 (4 teaspoons)

To prepare braised tofu, mix soy sauce, brown sugar, water, and sesame oil together. Set aside. Heat a medium-sized nonstick frying pan on medium-high heat. Brown cubes in frying pan 5 minutes, turning to brown all sides. Add soy sauce mixture to frying pan and sauté on high 1 minute, turning tofu to make sure all sides absorb sauce. Place on a large serving platter.

To make broth, place all the ingredients in a saucepan. Bring to a boil and cook 10 minutes, uncovered. Meanwhile, prepare vegetables. Wash bok choy and slice on the diagonal in 1-inch pieces; place on serving platter. Wash mushrooms and cut into quarters (cut into sixths if large); place on serving platter. Trim and string snow peas; add to platter. Place Chinese noodles on the platter and set platter on table.

To prepare dipping sauce, mix all the ingredients together and divide evenly among 4 large soup bowls. Place a bowl in front of each person.

 Recipe continues on page 103

FOODS OF THE
FAR EAST

HELPFUL HINTS

► *Tofu, also called soy bean curd, and fresh Chinese steamed egg noodles can be found in the refrigerated section of the produce department in most supermarkets. Dried Chinese steamed egg noodles, found in the ethnic foods section of supermarkets, may be used instead of fresh.*

► *To chop gingerroot quickly, peel it, cut it into small pieces, and press it through a garlic press with large holes.*

To cook, place the heating unit on the table on a heatproof mat. Pour the boiling broth into a fondue pot or saucepan and place on heating unit. Using either chopsticks or a fork, add several pieces of bok choy, mushrooms, snow peas, and braised tofu to the broth. Cook about 2 minutes and remove with chopsticks or with a slotted spoon. Dip pieces in sauce and eat. Continue until the platter is nearly finished, then add noodles and remaining vegetables and tofu to broth. Cook about 3 to 4 minutes, or until noodles are cooked through. Ladle into bowls containing remaining dipping sauce and enjoy the soup.

VARIATION: If you do not have a fondue pot or electric or gas burner, make the dish into a soup on the stovetop. In a saucepan, bring the vegetable broth and water to a boil. Add carrots and onions and simmer 10 minutes. Prepare all ingredients, including braised tofu, as described for fondue-style method. Add noodles, vegetables, and tofu to broth. Cook 3 to 4 minutes. Divide dipping sauce among 4 large soup bowls, pour soup in, and serve.

PICTURED:

Chinese Steamboat

SWEET AND SOUR MUSHROOMS *with* CHINESE RICE AND SCALLIONS

C O U N T D O W N

❶ Start rice.
❷ Make sweet and sour mushrooms.
❸ Finish rice.

SHOPPING LIST

½ pound fresh bean sprouts

1 small bunch scallions

¾ pound sliced or whole
portobello mushrooms

2 medium green bell peppers

One 16-ounce bag
fresh pineapple cubes

2 ripe medium tomatoes
(1 pound)

STAPLES

Large eggs (3)

Low-salt soy sauce

Cornstarch

Long-grain white rice

Sesame oil

Oriental rice wine vinegar

Sugar

Salt

Black peppercorns

SERVES 4
This meal contains
546 calories per serving,
with 29 percent
of calories from fat.

his dish has an interesting contrast and harmony of flavors and textures. The sweet and sour sauce is very light, not too sugary, and just coats the vegetables. ¶ The secret to making Chinese rice is to wash the rice grains carefully and then to let the rice mature for 10 minutes after it has finished cooking. This allows the rice to develop its texture and flavor.

SWEET AND SOUR MUSHROOMS

SAUCE
½ cup Oriental rice wine vinegar
1 tablespoon sugar
2 tablespoons low-salt soy sauce
½ teaspoon cornstarch

VEGETABLES
½ cup cornstarch, divided
¾ pound portobello mushrooms, washed,
    sliced, and cut in half (about 6 cups)
3 large egg whites
¼ cup sesame oil
2 medium green bell peppers, cut into
    1-inch dice (2 cups)
2 cups fresh pineapple cubes, drained
2 ripe medium tomatoes, cut into 2-inch dice
    (2 cups)

In a large bowl, mix sauce ingredients together, and set aside. Place ¼ cup of the cornstarch in another large bowl, add sliced mushrooms and toss. In a third bowl, break up egg whites with a fork. Add mushroom mixture to egg whites and toss. Place remaining ¼ cup cornstarch in the empty bowl and toss mushrooms again in cornstarch. In a wok or frying pan, heat sesame oil on high heat until smoking. Place mushrooms in pan and stir-fry 3 minutes. Add green bell peppers and stir-fry 2 minutes. Add pineapple, tomato, and sauce and toss constantly for 2 minutes. Serve over warm rice.

CHINESE RICE AND SCALLIONS

1 cup uncooked long-grain white rice
1½ cups water
8 scallions, sliced (2 cups)
2 cups fresh bean sprouts
2 teaspoons sesame oil
Salt and freshly ground black pepper to taste

Place rice in a strainer and rinse well, rubbing grains between your fingers. Place in a large saucepan, add water, cover, and bring to a boil. Remove cover, stir, lower heat to medium, cover, and continue to boil, 10 minutes. Remove cover and stir to make sure no rice sticks to pan. If rice is still very moist, simmer uncovered until only a few drops of moisture remain. Add scallions, bean sprouts, oil, and salt and pepper to taste. Cover and let stand 10 minutes. Loosen grains before serving.

FOODS OF THE
FAR EAST

HELPFUL HINTS

➤ *Buy fresh pineapple cubes in the produce department of the supermarket.*

➤ *Oriental rice wine vinegar, white rice vinegar, or seasoned rice vinegar can be found in the ethnic foods section of the supermarket. Use whichever one is available.*

➤ *Buy a good-quality sesame oil. A good-flavored oil is important to this dish.*

➤ *If you can't find sliced portobello mushrooms, buy whole ones and slice them. Any type of mushroom may be substituted for the portobellos.*

➤ *Make sure your wok or frying pan is very hot before you start to stir-fry.*

FIVE-SPICE STIR-FRY
with QUICK FRIED RICE

COUNTDOWN

❶ Boil rice and coat with oil.
❷ Prepare vegetables.
❸ Make stir-fry.
❹ Finish rice.

SHOPPING LIST

¼ pound fresh bean sprouts

1 medium red bell pepper

1 small bunch scallions

One 15-ounce can whole baby corn

One 15-ounce can straw mushrooms

One 2-ounce package slivered almonds

1 small jar Chinese five-spice powder

One 9-ounce package frozen petite peas (4½ ounces needed)

STAPLES

Carrots

Celery

Garlic

Yellow onion

Low-salt soy sauce

Large egg

Vegetable broth (one 14½-ounce can)

Cornstarch

Long-grain white rice

Canola oil

Oriental rice wine vinegar

Sugar

Salt

Black peppercorns

SERVES 4

This meal contains 596 calories per serving, with 27 percent of calories from fat.

The exotic flavors of Chinese five-spice powder delicately glaze the vegetables in this dish. A coffee-colored mixture of star anise, cinnamon, cloves, fennel seed, and Szechwan peppercorns, this spice creates an exotic and pungent flavor. Quick fried rice flavored with scallions, peas, and bean sprouts makes a perfect side dish for this meal.

FIVE-SPICE STIR-FRY

SAUCE

½ cup plus I tablespoon vegetable broth, divided

3 tablespoons Oriental rice wine vinegar

I teaspoon Chinese five-spice powder

5 medium cloves garlic, crushed

2 tablespoons low-salt soy sauce

2 ounces slivered almonds (about ⅓ cup)

VEGETABLES

I teaspoon canola oil

½ medium yellow onion, sliced (1 cup)

I medium red bell pepper, sliced (1 cup)

2 medium stalks celery, sliced (1 cup)

2 medium carrots, sliced (1 cup)

One 15-ounce can straw mushrooms, drained (1 cup)

One 15-ounce can whole baby corn, drained and cut in half (2 cups)

I teaspoon cornstarch

To make the sauce, mix ½ cup of the vegetable broth, the vinegar, Chinese five-spice powder, garlic, and soy sauce together. Heat wok or large nonstick frying pan on high heat. Add almonds and toss until golden, about 30 seconds. Remove to a plate and set aside. Add oil and heat on high until smoking. Add onion, red bell pepper, celery, and carrots and stir-fry 3 minutes. Add mushrooms and corn and stir-fry 2 minutes. Remove to a bowl. Add sauce to wok and boil 3 minutes. In a bowl, whisk cornstarch with remaining 1 tablespoon broth and add to wok. Boil about 30 seconds to thicken sauce. Remove from heat and return vegetables to wok. Toss with sauce to coat vegetables. Serve over rice.

✳ **QUICK FRIED RICE**
recipe follows

HELPFUL HINTS

➤ *Chinese five-spice powder can be found in the spice section of the supermarket.*

➤ *Slice all vegetables in a food processor fitted with a thin slicing blade.*

➤ *Onion is used in both recipes. Slice all at once and use as needed.*

➤ *Two woks are needed for the two recipes. If you don't have two woks, you can use a wok for one dish and a nonstick frying pan for the other, or use two frying pans.*

➤ *Make sure your woks or frying pans are very hot before you start to stir-fry.*

QUICK FRIED RICE

1½ cups uncooked long-grain white rice

2 tablespoons canola oil, divided

¼ medium yellow onion, sliced (½ cup)

4 scallions, sliced (⅔ cup)

1 cup fresh bean sprouts

1 cup frozen petite peas

1 tablespoon low-salt soy sauce

2 teaspoons sugar

1 large egg

Salt and freshly ground black pepper to taste

Fill a large saucepan three-quarters full with water and bring to a boil. Add rice and boil 10 minutes, or until cooked through. Drain in a colander and stir in 1 tablespoon of the canola oil. While rice is cooking, arrange vegetables in order of use on one or more cutting boards. In a bowl, whisk the soy sauce and sugar together and set aside. Heat a wok or large nonstick frying pan on high heat and add the remaining 1 tablespoon oil. When oil is smoking, add onion and stir-fry 1 minute. Add scallions and continue to fry another 30 seconds. Add bean sprouts and rice and stir-fry 3 minutes. Using a wooden spoon, push the ingredients aside, making a depression in the center. Crack the egg into the hole, beating with a fork just to mix the yolk and white, then mix egg into the other ingredients. Make a depression in the center again and add sweetened soy sauce and peas. Toss all of the ingredients together and stir-fry another 3 minutes. Taste for seasoning and add salt and pepper, if desired.

FOODS OF THE
FAR EAST

PICTURED:

Five-Spice Stir-Fry with Quick Fried Rice

INDIAN SPICED SPINACH
with LENTIL AND RICE PILAF

COUNTDOWN

❶ Start lentils and rice.

❷ While lentils and rice cook, make spinach.

❸ Finish lentils and rice.

SHOPPING LIST

Two 10-ounce packages fresh prewashed spinach (20 ounces needed)

2 ripe medium tomatoes (1 pound)

One 12-ounce package lentils (7 ounces needed)

One 1¾-ounce package pine nuts (1 ounce needed)

Ground turmeric or saffron strands

STAPLES

Garlic

Yellow onions (3)

Butter or margarine

Vegetable broth (two 14½-ounce cans)

Raisins

Long-grain white rice

Olive oil spray

Cayenne pepper

Ground cardamom

Ground coriander

Ground cumin

Salt

Black peppercorns

SERVES 4

This meal contains 630 calories per serving, with 24 percent of calories from fat.

ardamom, coriander, and cumin add a taste of India to this spinach dish. Onions, pine nuts, and garlic complete the exciting ethnic flavors. In the past, I rarely used fresh spinach for a quick meal because it is difficult to wash. Now, with prewashed spinach available, using fresh spinach is a breeze. ¶ I like to use lentils because they do not need to be presoaked. A secret to cooking them quickly is to bring the liquid to a boil and slowly pour in the lentils so that the liquid continues to boil.

INDIAN SPICED SPINACH

Olive oil spray

1 medium yellow onion, sliced (2 cups)

2 medium cloves garlic, crushed

2 ripe medium tomatoes, cut into 1-inch cubes
   (2 cups)

20 ounces (16 cups) prewashed fresh spinach

2 teaspoons ground cumin

2 teaspoons ground coriander

2 teaspoons ground cardamom

¼ teaspoon cayenne pepper

¼ cup toasted pine nuts

4 teaspoons butter or margarine

Salt and freshly ground black pepper to taste

Prepare a large nonstick frying pan with olive oil spray and place on high heat. When frying pan is hot, add onions and sauté 10 minutes. Add garlic and sauté 1 minute. Add tomatoes and spinach, cover, and cook 5 minutes. Remove lid, add spices and pine nuts, and cook another 5 minutes, uncovered. Stir in butter until it melts. Add salt and pepper to taste. Spoon onto serving platter and serve with pilaf.

LENTIL AND RICE PILAF

Olive oil spray

2 medium yellow onions, sliced (4 cups)

4 cups vegetable broth

2 cups water

1 cup uncooked lentils

1 cup uncooked long-grain white rice

1 cup raisins

1 tablespoon ground turmeric or
   saffron strands

Salt and freshly ground black pepper to taste

Slice the onions in a food processor. Prepare a large nonstick frying pan with olive oil spray and place on high heat. When frying pan is hot, add onions and sauté 10 minutes. Remove onions to a plate. Combine broth and water in a large bowl. Place 4 cups of the liquid in the same frying pan and bring to a boil. Place lentils in a strainer and rinse under cold water, removing any stones you might find. Add lentils slowly to the boiling liquid so that the liquid continues to boil. Cover and cook 5 minutes. Add rice and the remaining 2 cups liquid. Cover and simmer on medium heat 20 minutes. Remove cover and continue to cook until liquid is absorbed, 5 minutes. Add onions, raisins, and turmeric. Stir to mix well. Remove from heat. Add salt and pepper to taste.

FOODS OF THE
FAR EAST

HELPFUL HINTS

➤ *All of the spices can be found in the spice section of the supermarket. Be sure yours are no more than 6 months old. Spices lose their flavor and strength if kept too long.*

➤ *Red lentils are best for this dish. If they are not available, use any type of lentil.*

➤ *Measure and prepare all the ingredients before you start to cook. Place them on cutting boards or in bowls ready to use.*

➤ *Onions are used in both recipes. Slice all at once and use as needed.*

➤ *Toast pine nuts in a toaster oven or preheat the broiler and toast on a baking tray under broiler.*

BLACK PEPPER "TENDERLOIN"
with SESAME NOODLES

COUNTDOWN

❶ Place water for noodles on to boil.
❷ Preheat oven to 200 degrees F.
❸ Make "tenderloin."
❹ Finish Sesame Noodles.

SHOPPING LIST

¼ pound shiitake mushrooms
2 medium red bell peppers
½ pound fresh or dried Chinese steamed egg noodles
12 ounces firm tofu
1 jar cracked black pepper

STAPLES

Low-salt soy sauce
All-purpose flour
Sesame oil
Sugar

SERVES 4
This meal contains 529 calories per serving, with 18 percent of calories from fat.

When I saw "tenderloin" on the Kum Tak Lam vegetarian menu in Hong Kong, I was more than surprised. When I tasted it, I was delighted. Tofu, mushrooms, and a soy sauce mixture give this dish the color and texture of beef tenderloin. It has an intriguing, light quality and lots of flavor. I created this dish with that memorable meal at Lau Wo Ching's Hong Kong restaurant in mind. As with most Chinese dishes, the preparation takes a little time, but the actual cooking time is very short.

BLACK PEPPER "TENDERLOIN" WITH SESAME NOODLES

½ pound uncooked fresh or dried Chinese
   steamed egg noodles

4 teaspoons sesame oil, divided

½ cup low-salt soy sauce

½ cup sugar

¾ tablespoon cracked black pepper

12 ounces firm tofu

¼ pound shiitake mushrooms, coarsely
   chopped (1½ cups)

1 cup all-purpose flour

2 medium red bell peppers, thinly sliced
   (2 cups)

Place a large pot with 3 to 4 quarts of water on to boil for noodles. Preheat oven to 200 degrees F. When water is boiling, add noodles and cook 1 minute if fresh, 3 minutes if dried. Drain noodles in colander, return to pot and toss with 2 teaspoons of the sesame oil. Spread noodles in a pie plate and place in the oven to keep warm. In a medium-sized bowl, mix soy sauce, sugar, and cracked pepper together, making sure sugar is dissolved. Set aside. To make the tenderloin, chop tofu, mushrooms, and flour in a food processor fitted with the metal chopping blade. Or, chop tofu and mushrooms by hand and blend in flour. Remove from bowl and using your hands, press together to form a firm ball. Roll ball into the shape of a tube about 10 inches long and 2 inches in diameter. Place on a cutting board and cut into ¼-inch slices (if too thick, flatten with palm of hand). Heat remaining 2 teaspoons sesame oil in a large nonstick frying pan on high heat until smoking. Place tofu slices in frying pan and brown on both sides, about 1 minute per side. Remove to a plate or cutting board. Lower heat and add red bell peppers and soy sauce mixture to frying pan. Simmer gently 2 minutes. Remove bell peppers with slotted spoon, leaving sauce in frying pan. Add tofu slices to pan and simmer 1 minute, then turn slices and simmer 2 minutes more. Remove noodles from oven, spoon bell peppers over top, and layer tofu slices on peppers. Spoon sauce over top.

FOODS OF THE
FAR EAST

HELPFUL HINTS

➤ *Tofu, also called soy bean curd, and fresh Chinese steamed egg noodles can be found in the refrigerated section of the produce department in most supermarkets.*

➤ *Dried Chinese steamed egg noodles can be used instead of fresh and are sold in the ethnic foods section of supermarkets.*

➤ *Green bell peppers can be substituted for red bell peppers.*

➤ *Cracked black pepper can be found in the spice section of the supermarket.*

➤ *Use a sharp knife to slice the tofu. If your slices are too thick, simply flatten them with the palm of your hand.*

VEGETABLE CURRY
with TOASTED RICE PILAF

COUNTDOWN

❶ Make rice.

❷ While rice cooks, prepare vegetable curry.

SHOPPING LIST

¾ pound eggplant

2 medium red bell peppers

1 pound zucchini

1 small jar mango chutney

One 32-ounce bottle apple juice

1 small package curry powder

STAPLES

Garlic

Red onions (2)

Butter or margarine

All-purpose flour

White basmati rice

Ground cumin

Salt

Black peppercorns

SERVES 4

This meal contains 745 calories per serving, with 8 percent of calories from fat.

W hen eggplant, tomatoes, zucchini, and bell peppers are at their peak in autumn, I like to use them in as many ways as possible. I cut the eggplant into small cubes to help it cook faster. The rest of the vegetables can be sliced in a food processor. ¶ The curry powder sold in supermarkets is a blend of about 15 herbs, spices, and seeds. This type of powder loses its flavor quickly. If your curry powder has been sitting on your spice shelf for longer than six months, buy a new one. The dish will taste much better if you do.

VEGETABLE CURRY

4 teaspoons butter or margarine, divided

2 medium red onions, sliced (4 cups)

¾ pound eggplant, unpeeled, cut into ½-inch dice (4 cups)

2 medium zucchini, sliced (4 cups)

2 medium red bell peppers, sliced (2 cups)

4 medium cloves garlic, crushed

½ cup mango chutney

½ cup all-purpose flour

8 teaspoons ground cumin

1½ tablespoons curry powder

4 cups water

Salt and freshly ground black pepper to taste

Heat 2 teaspoons of the butter in a nonstick frying pan on medium heat. Add onions and eggplant and sauté 5 minutes. Add zucchini, red bell peppers, and garlic and sauté 5 minutes more. Push vegetables to sides of pan and add remaining butter and the chutney to cleared center of frying pan. Add flour, cumin, and curry powder. Mix well. Add water and toss vegetables. Cook until sauce thickens, about 1 minute. Add salt and pepper to taste.

TOASTED RICE PILAF

4 teaspoons butter or margarine

1½ cups uncooked white basmati rice

4 cups apple juice

Salt and freshly ground black pepper to taste

Heat butter in a large nonstick frying pan. Add rice and sauté 2 minutes, until golden brown. Add apple juice, bring to a simmer, and cover. Simmer 15 minutes. All of the liquid will be absorbed and the rice will be cooked and crisp on the outside. Add salt and pepper to taste.

FOODS OF THE
FAR EAST

HELPFUL HINTS

➤ *Long-grain or Texmati white rice can be substituted for white basmati rice.*

➤ *Use any good-quality bottled mango chutney.*

CAJUN

AND

CARIBBEAN

CUISINE

CAJUN KABOBS *with* CREOLE RICE AND RED BEANS

COUNTDOWN

❶ Preheat broiler.

❷ Place water for rice on to boil.

❸ Place aluminum foil–lined baking tray in broiler.

❹ Start rice.

❺ Skewer and cook kabobs.

❻ Finish rice.

SHOPPING LIST

2 small eggplants (1 pound)

1 pound mushrooms (about 12 to 16 medium mushrooms)

2 medium yellow squash (12 ounces)

One 19-ounce can small red kidney beans

One 28-ounce can crushed tomatoes (18 ounces needed)

1 package wooden skewers, if needed

STAPLES

Garlic

Yellow onion

Hot pepper sauce

Worcestershire sauce

Vegetable broth (one 14½-ounce can)

Long-grain white rice

Olive oil

Olive oil spray

Cayenne pepper

Dried oregano

Dried thyme

Paprika

Salt

Black peppercorns

SERVES 4

This meal contains 586 calories per serving, with 16 percent of calories from fat.

Simple ingredients, hot spices, and long, slow cooking are the key elements of Cajun cooking. For a quick dinner, I've created a spice mixture that captures the vivid flavors of Cajun cooking without requiring the usual long cooking time. If it's grilling weather and you have a gas grill, the kabobs take no time at all. Red beans and rice, basic Creole fare, complement the spice of the kabobs.

CAJUN KABOBS

Olive oil spray
4 teaspoons olive oil
4 teaspoons paprika
½ teaspoon cayenne pepper
1 teaspoon dried oregano
1 teaspoon dried thyme
1 teaspoon salt
½ teaspoon freshly ground black pepper
2 small eggplants (1 pound)
2 medium yellow squash (12 ounces)
1 pound mushrooms
8 skewers

Preheat broiler. Line a baking tray with aluminum foil and spray with olive oil spray. Place on oven rack about 5 inches from heat. Mix olive oil, paprika, cayenne, oregano, thyme, salt, and black pepper together in a small bowl. Wash eggplant and squash and cut into 2-inch pieces. Wash mushrooms and leave whole or cut in half if large. Toss vegetables in spice mixture. Place vegetables on skewers, alternating vegetables for variety. Remove baking tray from oven and place skewers on foil. Return to oven and broil 4 minutes. Turn and broil 4 minutes more. Remove and serve.

CREOLE RICE AND RED BEANS

4 teaspoons olive oil
2 medium yellow onions, sliced (4 cups)
6 medium cloves garlic, crushed
1 cup uncooked long-grain white rice
2 cups vegetable broth
2 cups canned crushed tomatoes
2 cups canned red kidney beans
Several drops hot pepper sauce
2 tablespoons Worcestershire sauce
Salt and freshly ground black pepper to taste

Heat olive oil in a medium-sized nonstick frying pan on high heat. Add onion and garlic and sauté 1 minute. Add rice and sauté 1 minute more. Add broth and tomatoes. Bring to a boil, cover, lower heat to medium-high, and simmer 15 minutes. Meanwhile, drain and rinse beans. Add to rice with hot pepper sauce and Worcestershire sauce. Simmer several minutes. Taste and add more pepper sauce or Worcestershire as desired. Add salt and pepper to taste. Serve on individual plates with kabobs.

CAJUN
AND
CARIBBEAN
CUISINE

HELPFUL HINTS

➤ *Canned small red kidney beans can be found in most supermarkets. The smaller size gives a better texture to the dish, but regular red beans can also be used.*

➤ *Spices lose their flavor and strength if kept too long If yours are more than 6 months old, it's time for a new bottle.*

➤ *Warm the beans and vegetable broth in a microwave oven to save cooking and clean-up time.*

➤ *If you're using a broiler, preheating a baking tray speeds up the cooking time. Line the baking tray with aluminum foil to save clean-up time.*

AUNT HELEN ROSE'S GUMBO *with* AVOCADO AND GRAPEFRUIT SALAD

C O U N T D O W N

❶ Place water for rice on to boil.
❷ Make gumbo.
❸ While gumbo cooks, make rice.
❹ Make salad.

SHOPPING LIST

1 small ripe avocado (½ pound)
2 medium grapefruits
1 small head red lettuce (4 cups)
2 medium green bell peppers
One 14½-ounce can whole tomatoes (6 ounces needed)
1 small jar filé powder
One 9-ounce package frozen corn (4 ounces needed)
One 10-ounce package frozen lima beans (4 ounces needed)
One 16-ounce package frozen cut okra

STAPLES

Celery
Garlic
Yellow onion
Dijon mustard
Honey
Hot pepper sauce
Worcestershire sauce
Nonfat plain yogurt
All-purpose flour
Long-grain white rice
Canola oil
Olive oil spray
Cayenne pepper
Dried thyme
Salt
Black peppercorns

SERVES 4
This meal contains 583 calories per serving, with 27 percent of calories from fat.

My husband always talks longingly about his Aunt Helen Rose's gumbo. I still laugh thinking about the first time I met his family, and they greeted me with, "We're having gumbo tonight." On a recent visit with Helen Rose, I mentioned that I wish I could make her famous dish, but that it takes too long. She sent me this quick version. My husband's verdict? It's great. ¶ Don't worry about the number of ingredients. Slice all of the vegetables in a food processor, and the rest goes quickly. The key to a good gumbo is cooking the oil and flour together to form a rich, light brown roux. ¶ This gumbo improves with age. If you have time, make extra and use it a second night, or freeze it for a future quick dinner.

CAJUN AND CARIBBEAN CUISINE

AUNT HELEN ROSE'S GUMBO

Olive oil spray

One 16-ounce package frozen cut okra
(4 cups)

¾ medium yellow onion, thinly sliced
(1½ cups)

1½ medium green bell peppers, sliced
(1½ cups)

3 medium stalks celery, sliced (1½ cups)

6 medium cloves garlic, crushed

1½ tablespoons canola oil

3 tablespoons all-purpose flour

4 cups water

1½ teaspoons dried thyme

¼ teaspoon cayenne pepper

¾ cup canned whole tomatoes, with liquid

¾ cup frozen corn or drained canned corn

¾ cup frozen baby lima beans

1½ tablespoons Worcestershire sauce

3 tablespoons filé powder

Salt and freshly ground black pepper to taste

Worcestershire sauce, for serving

Hot pepper sauce, for serving

Prepare a large nonstick saucepan with
olive oil spray and heat on medium-high
heat. Add okra, onion, bell peppers, celery,
and garlic. Sauté 5 minutes. Remove vegetables to a bowl. Add oil to saucepan and
stir in flour. Sauté 3 minutes, until flour
turns a cocoa color. Add the 4 cups water
little by little, stirring constantly until
smooth. Bring to a simmer. Add thyme and
cayenne. Add tomatoes, breaking them up
with a spoon. Return vegetables to the pan
and simmer 5 minutes. Add corn and lima

beans. Continue to simmer 5 minutes. Turn
off heat, add Worcestershire sauce, filé
powder, and salt and pepper to taste, and
let stand while making the rice. Serve the
gumbo with Worcestershire sauce and hot
pepper sauce at the table to add as desired.

FLUFFY RICE

1 cup uncooked long-grain white rice
Salt and freshly ground black pepper to taste

Bring a large pot filled with 2 to 3 quarts of
water to a boil. Add rice and boil, uncovered, about 10 minutes. Test a grain. Rice
should be cooked through, but not soft.
Drain rice in a colander. Run hot water
through rice and stir with a fork. Add salt
and pepper to taste. Divide among 4 large
soup bowls, spoon gumbo over the top,
and serve.

* AVOCADO AND GRAPEFRUIT
SALAD *recipe follows*

HELPFUL HINTS

➤ *Buy frozen cut okra, or
use fresh.*

➤ *Use a food processor to
slice onions, green peppers,
and celery.*

➤ *For Fluffy Rice, boil rice
as you would pasta, in a
pot large enough to let the
grains roll freely in the
boiling water.*

AVOCADO AND GRAPEFRUIT SALAD

¼ cup nonfat plain yogurt

2 tablespoons Dijon mustard

1 tablespoon honey

2 grapefruits, sliced in half across segments

1 small ripe avocado (½ pound), peeled, seeded, and sliced (1 cup)

½ small head red lettuce (2 cups)

To make dressing, mix yogurt, mustard, and honey together in a medium-sized bowl. To prepare grapefruits, with a serrated knife, cut around grapefruit between peel and fruit, making sure the knife touches the base of the fruit. Remove fruit and slice into 2-inch pieces. Add grapefruit and avocado to bowl with dressing and toss. Wash and dry lettuce and place on a serving platter. Spoon grapefruit and avocado on lettuce.

CAJUN
AND
CARIBBEAN
CUISINE

PICTURED:

Aunt Helen Rose's Gumbo with Avocado and Grapefruit Salad

ARROZ CON GARBANZO (SPANISH RICE AND BEANS)
with TOSSED GREENS

C O U N T D O W N

❶ Preheat oven to 350 degrees F to warm bread.
❷ Make rice and beans.
❸ While rice cooks, make salad.

SHOPPING LIST

1 medium cucumber

1 small head Bibb lettuce

1 ripe medium tomato (½ pound)

One 19-ounce can chickpeas

One 8-ounce jar pitted black olives

Two 7½-ounce jars sliced red pimientos

1 small package saffron strands

1 loaf Cuban bread

One 9-ounce package frozen petite peas

STAPLES

Celery

Garlic

Yellow onions (2)

Dijon mustard

Vegetable broth (three 14½-ounce cans)

Long-grain white rice

Olive oil

Dry sherry

Salt

Black peppercorns

SERVES 4

This meal contains 765 calories per serving, with 21 percent of calories from fat.

This dish is made by cooking the rice in a frying pan, where it absorbs the flavors of the saffron, garlic, sherry, vegetables, and herbs. A secret is to sauté the garbanzo beans until they are crisp and you hear them pop. ¶ A tossed green salad and warm Cuban bread complete this Spanish meal. If you're pressed for time, use any salad vegetables you have on hand and your favorite low-fat dressing, or make the quick and easy Tossed Greens that follows. ¶ The rice dish will keep overnight in the refrigerator. If you have time, double the recipe, freeze half, and you will have another quick meal ready.

ARROZ CON GARBANZO (SPANISH RICE AND BEANS)

2 tablespoons olive oil

One 19-ounce can chickpeas, drained and rinsed (2 cups)

½ teaspoon cayenne pepper

1 medium yellow onion, diced (2 cups)

10 medium cloves garlic, crushed

1 cup uncooked long-grain white rice

1½ teaspoons saffron strands

2 cups vegetable broth

1 cup dry sherry

1 ripe medium tomato, diced (1 cup)

Two 7½-ounce cans sliced red pimientos, drained and diced (1 cup)

1 cup frozen petite peas

20 pitted black olives, cut in half

1 loaf Cuban bread

Salt and freshly ground black pepper to taste

Preheat oven to 350 degrees F. Heat olive oil in a large nonstick frying pan. Add chickpeas and cayenne and sauté on high 1 minute. Remove to a plate, lower heat to medium-high, add onion and garlic, and sauté 5 minutes. Add rice to frying pan. Sauté a few seconds. Sprinkle saffron over rice and add broth. Bring to a simmer and add sherry, tomato, and pimientos. Return chickpeas to frying pan. Cover and simmer 15 minutes. Add peas and olives and cook 1 minute. Add salt and pepper to taste. Place bread in oven to warm through, 5 to 7 minutes.

TOSSED GREENS

2 teaspoons red wine vinegar

4 teaspoons Dijon mustard

1 tablespoon diced yellow onion

¼ cup vegetable broth

4 teaspoons olive oil

1 small head Bibb lettuce (4 cups)

1 small cucumber, peeled and sliced (1½ cups)

4 medium stalks celery, sliced (2 cups)

Salt and freshly ground black pepper to taste

To make dressing, whisk vinegar and mustard together in a salad bowl. Add onion and mix thoroughly. Add broth and oil and season with salt and pepper. For salad, wash and drain lettuce leaves, tear into bite-sized pieces, and add to bowl. Add cucumber and celery to bowl and toss with dressing.

CAJUN
AND
CARIBBEAN
CUISINE

HELPFUL HINTS

➤ *Chickpeas are also called garbanzo beans.*

➤ *Any olive oil can be used in the recipe, but Spanish olive oil adds a slightly peppery flavor to the dish.*

➤ *Bijol can be used instead of saffron. It is made from ground annatto seed and often contains some cumin and oregano. Turmeric can also be substituted.*

➤ *Any type of lettuce can be used, or buy prewashed salad.*

➤ *Cuban bread is available in the bread section of the supermarket. Any type of bread can be used.*

➤ *Onion is used in both recipes. Dice all at once and use as needed.*

JAMBALAYA *with*
ROMAINE AND ORANGE SALAD

C O U N T D O W N

❶ Start onions and flour. While they cook, prepare other vegetables.

❷ When flour is ready, complete jambalaya preparations.

❸ While jambalaya is cooking, make salad.

SHOPPING LIST

2 medium red bell peppers

One 10-ounce package prewashed lettuce (8 ounces needed) or 1 small head romaine lettuce

1 medium orange

2 ripe medium tomatoes (1 pound)

One 16-ounce package frozen cut okra

STAPLES

Celery

Garlic

Yellow onion

Dijon mustard

Hot pepper sauce

Vegetable broth (two 14½-ounce cans)

All-purpose flour

Long-grain white rice

Canola oil

Red wine vinegar

Cayenne pepper

Dried thyme

Salt

Black peppercorns

SERVES 4

This meal contains 461 calories per serving, with 27 percent of calories from fat.

This is hearty Cajun country cooking as it's served on the bayous of Louisiana. Serve it the way the locals do, with hot pepper sauce placed right on the table. The secret is to cook the oil and flour roux until it is a tan, café au lait color. ¶ A little orange added to the salad is a refreshing touch with this hot and spicy dinner. Try the low-fat dressing recipe or, if you're pressed for time, use your favorite bottled low-fat dressing.

JAMBALAYA

3 tablespoons canola oil

¼ medium yellow onion, sliced (½ cup)

⅓ cup all-purpose flour

4 medium cloves garlic, crushed

One 16-ounce package frozen cut okra
  (4 cups)

4 medium celery stalks, sliced (2 cups)

2 medium red bell peppers, diced (2 cups)

1 cup uncooked long-grain white rice

½ teaspoon cayenne pepper

½ teaspoon freshly ground black pepper

½ teaspoon dried thyme, or 1 teaspoon
  fresh thyme

3 cups vegetable broth

2 ripe medium tomatoes, diced (2 cups)

2 tablespoons red wine vinegar

Salt to taste

Hot pepper sauce, for serving

Heat oil in large nonstick frying pan on medium-low heat. Add onions and sauté 30 seconds. Lower heat and stir in flour. Continue to sauté 10 minutes, letting flour turn a light tan color (do not let it turn black). Add garlic, okra, celery, and red bell peppers and sauté 5 minutes, until vegetables are wilted. Stir in rice, cayenne pepper, black pepper, and thyme. Add broth and stir well. Cover and simmer 15 minutes. Fold in tomatoes and vinegar, and add salt to taste. Spoon onto plates, serve, and pass the hot pepper sauce.

✳ **ROMAINE AND ORANGE SALAD**
  recipe follows

CAJUN
AND
CARIBBEAN
CUISINE

HELPFUL HINTS

➤ *To speed up preparation, slice the vegetables in a food processor.*

➤ *Frozen cut okra is best, though fresh okra can be used. Look for young tender okra when buying it fresh and discard tops when slicing.*

ROMAINE AND ORANGE SALAD

8 ounces prewashed lettuce, or ½ small head
   romaine lettuce (4 cups)
1 medium orange

DRESSING
2 tablespoons vegetable broth
2 tablespoons fresh orange juice
2 tablespoons Dijon mustard
2 teaspoons canola oil
Salt and freshly ground black pepper to taste

Wash romaine lettuce and tear into bite-
sized pieces. Over a small bowl, remove
orange peel and cut into segments, reserving as much juice as possible. Cut segments
in half and set aside. Whisk broth, 2 tablespoons of the orange juice, and the mustard
together in a salad bowl. Whisk in oil. Add
salt and pepper to taste. Add lettuce and
orange segments and toss.

CAJUN
AND
CARIBBEAN
CUISINE

PICTURED:

*Jambalaya with
Romaine and Orange Salad*

JAMAICAN OKRA STEW *with* WEST INDIAN CHRISTOPHENE SALAD

C O U N T D O W N

❶ Place water for rice on to boil.
❷ Place water for chayote on to boil.
❸ Start okra stew.
❹ While stew cooks, start rice.
❺ While both cook, make salad.

SHOPPING LIST

2 chayote (christophenes)
1 medium green bell pepper
2 medium jalapeño peppers
1 small bunch scallions
2 ripe medium tomatoes
(1 pound)
1 small bunch fresh thyme
1 small bunch fresh parsley
Three 14½-ounce cans stewed
tomatoes (36 ounces needed)
One 16-ounce package
frozen black-eyed peas
(10 ounces needed)
One 10-ounce package
frozen corn
One 16-ounce package frozen
cut okra (8 ounces needed)

STAPLES

Garlic
Red onion
Dijon mustard
Butter or margarine
Long-grain white rice
Canola oil
Red wine vinegar
Cayenne pepper
Ground allspice
Salt
Black peppercorns

SERVES 4
This meal contains
576 calories per serving,
with 15 percent
of calories from fat.

Creole meets Caribbean in this spicy stew. While exploring the bustling open food market in Montego Bay, chef Louis Bailey told me that scallions, thyme, and pimiento (allspice) are important in Jamaican cooking, but scotch bonnet is the essential ingredient. ¶ Scotch bonnet is one of the hottest peppers known. It's small and looks a little like a tiny pumpkin. I've seen brightly colored red, green, orange, and yellow scotch bonnet. It can be difficult to find, however, so I have used jalapeño peppers for this recipe. You can use any type of hot pepper, selecting it according to the level of heat you prefer. ¶ Chayote, also known as christophene or cho-cho, is eaten raw or cooked. Its crunch is a nice contrast to the tomatoes.

JAMAICAN OKRA STEW

2 tablespoons butter or margarine

1 medium green bell pepper, sliced (1 cup)

2 cups frozen cut okra

4 cups canned stewed tomatoes, with liquid

2 cups frozen black-eyed peas

2 medium jalapeño peppers, seeded and
  chopped (2 tablespoons)

2 cups frozen or drained canned corn

¼ cup fresh thyme, or 2 tablespoons
  dried thyme

¾ teaspoon ground allspice

Salt to taste

6 scallions, sliced (1 cup), for garnish

Melt butter in a large nonstick frying pan.
Sauté green bell pepper and okra for 2
minutes on medium-high heat. Lower heat
to medium-low, add tomatoes, black-eyed
peas, and jalapeño peppers, and cook,
covered, 25 minutes. Remove cover, add
corn, thyme, and allspice, and cook 1
minute. Add salt to taste. Remove from
heat and serve over boiled rice with
scallions sprinkled on top.

FLUFFY RICE

1 cup uncooked long-grain white rice
Salt and freshly ground black pepper to taste

Bring 3 to 4 quarts of water to a boil,
add rice, and cook, uncovered, about 10
minutes. Test a grain. Rice should be
cooked through, but not soft. Drain rice

in a colander. Run hot water through rice
and stir with a fork. Add salt and pepper to
taste. Divide among 4 large soup bowls and
spoon okra stew over the top.

WEST INDIAN
CHRISTOPHENE SALAD

2 tablespoons red wine vinegar

1 tablespoon Dijon mustard

2 teaspoons canola oil

2 tablespoons water

2 medium cloves garlic, crushed

¼ teaspoon cayenne pepper

2 chayotes (christophenes)

2 ripe medium tomatoes, diced (2 cups)

½ medium red onion, diced (1 cup)

½ cup chopped fresh parsley, for garnish

Place 1 quart of water on to boil in a double
boiler. To make dressing, whisk vinegar
and mustard together in a small bowl.
Add oil and whisk to blend until smooth.
Add water, garlic, and cayenne and mix
well. Set aside. Wash chayotes and cut in
half from narrow end to base. Remove pit
and cut into strips. Steam chayotes in a
double boiler 3 to 4 minutes, then place on
a serving platter, overlapping slices.
Sprinkle tomatoes and onions over top.
Spoon dressing over vegetables and
sprinkle parsley on top.

CAJUN
AND
CARIBBEAN
CUISINE

HELPFUL HINT

➤ *Frozen cut okra is best,
though fresh okra can
be used. Look for young
tender okra when buying
it fresh, and discard tops
when slicing.*

BAJAN MACARONI PIE *with* ISLAND BEET AND CARROT SALAD

COUNTDOWN

❶ Place water for pasta on to boil.
❷ Sauté onion and green peppers.
❸ Prepare remaining macaroni ingredients.
❹ Prepare salad while macaroni sets.

SHOPPING LIST

2 medium green bell peppers
One 8-ounce package shredded sharp Cheddar cheese
One 16-ounce container nonfat ricotta cheese
One 16-ounce can sliced beets
One 16-ounce box small elbow macaroni (12 ounces needed)

STAPLES

Carrots
Yellow onion
Dijon mustard
Hot pepper sauce
Olive oil
Olive oil spray
Distilled white vinegar
Salt
Black peppercorns

SERVES 4
This meal contains
723 calories per serving,
with 28 percent
of calories from fat.

t is probably the strong English influence on Barbados that prompted this island favorite. During my visit to this sunny, tropical European haven, I was surprised to discover that the locals hold contests at Christmas to find the best macaroni pie. This pie won for its rich creaminess.

BAJAN MACARONI PIE

12 ounces uncooked small elbow macaroni
(3 cups)

Olive oil spray

1 medium yellow onion, grated (2 cups)

2 medium green bell peppers, grated (2 cups)

2 cups nonfat ricotta cheese

8 ounces shredded sharp Cheddar cheese
(2 cups)

Several drops hot pepper sauce

Salt and freshly ground black pepper to taste

Place a large pot filled with 3 to 4 quarts
water on to boil. When water boils, add
macaroni and boil 10 minutes. Meanwhile,
prepare a large nonstick frying pan with
olive oil spray and place on medium heat.
Add onion and green bell peppers and
sauté 5 minutes. Combine ricotta and half
the Cheddar cheese in a large bowl. Add
hot pepper sauce and mix in onion and
green bell peppers. Drain macaroni in a
colander and add to cheese mixture. Add
salt and pepper to taste. Return to frying
pan and sprinkle remaining Cheddar evenly
over the top. Cover and let set 10 minutes
on medium heat.

ISLAND BEET AND CARROT SALAD

2 cups sliced canned beets

4 medium carrots, grated (2 cups)

DRESSING

2 tablespoons distilled white vinegar

4 teaspoons Dijon mustard

2 teaspoons olive oil

Salt and freshly ground black pepper

Drain beet slices and arrange in a circle on
a serving plate. Spoon grated carrots into
center of plate. In a small bowl, mix vinegar and mustard together. Blend in oil and
add salt and pepper to taste. Spoon over
carrots and beets.

CAJUN AND CARIBBEAN
CUISINE

HELPFUL HINTS

➤ *Buy shredded Cheddar cheese.*

➤ *To save clean-up time, grate onion and bell peppers together in a food processor fitted with a grating blade. Remove onion and bell peppers and grate carrots in same bowl.*

VEGETARIAN DISHES AND WINE *By Fred Tasker, whose weekly wine column is carried in the* Miami Herald *and other newspapers across the United States.*

Now that so many doctors recognize the health benefits of moderate wine consumption, cooks are taking new interest in devising good matches of wine and vegetarian meals.

Now, red meat with red wine, white meat with white wine obviously doesn't apply here. And red beans with red wine or white beans with white wine would be silly. So where do we start? Maybe with the assertion that vegetarian dishes take on much of their flavor not from the veggies themselves, but from the herbs, oils, spices, and sauces they're cooked in.

So the old principles can apply: Spicy dishes go nicely with white wines that are slightly sweet—chenin blanc, riesling, gewürztraminer—or full-bodied, full-flavored whites like viognier, fiano di avelino, or white Rioja. They also go well with red wines that are a bit spicy— zinfandel, Côtes du Rhône—or fruity reds like Beaujolais, pinot noir, barbera, young "crianza"-style Rioja.

Green veggies—from broccoli to brussels sprouts— that are simply steamed and dressed with butter or oil go nicely with sauvignon blanc. Its crisp, herbal qualities match the flavors, cut the oils.

Tomato sauces and cooked green bell peppers are high in acid, calling for high-acid whites like sauvignon blanc or high-acid reds like Chianti. The charcoal flavor of grilled vegetables—from eggplant to portobello mushrooms—are naturals with most red wines.

Most cream or mild cheese sauces can go with rich white wines like California chardonnay, Australia's new semillon/chardonnay blends, or Washington's semillon/sauvignon blanc blends, or, again, with those light, fruity reds. Stronger cheese sauces with, say, Cheddar can take even a bolder, more tannic red cabernet sauvignon.

Vegetable dishes heavy with olive oil can also take a fairly tannic red wine, for the same reason a steak would—the tannin strips the fatty-oily flavor from your mouth, refreshing it for the next bite. A high-acid white like sauvignon blanc can do the same job.

Finally, never forget the most important rule of all food-wine matches.

Life is short. Drink what you like.

[PICTURED: *Roasted Red Pepper Pasta with Sautéed Escarole and Chickpeas, page 36*]

SPECIFIC WINE RECOMMENDATIONS

FLAVORS OF THE MEDITERRANEAN

➤ Orzo and Three-Cheese "Risotto" with Tomato and Onion Salad

The sweet richness of this dish cries out for a lush, fruity red wine like French Beaujolais or a young, "crainza"-style Spanish Rioja.

➤ Tabbouleh with Toasted Walnut Couscous

This is packed with herbal, vegetal flavors of mint, parsley, scallions; why not pair it with an herbal California sauvignon blanc, or its French counterpart, sancerre or pouilly fumé.

MODERN AMERICAN COMFORT FOODS

➤ Ricotta Soufflé with Tomato Bruschetta

With both sweetness and richness, this goes nicely with a white chenin blanc. Interestingly, both the dry, full-bodied French-style chenin blanc and the slightly sweeter California style are equally good matches.

➤ Mushroom Stroganoff with Buttered Egg Noodles and Lima Beans

This dish is hugely rich. I matched it with a red pinot noir and it wasn't big enough. I turned to a muscular but sweetly tannic cabernet sauvignon and it was wonderful.

TEX-MEX AND SOUTHWESTERN CUISINE

➤ Goat Cheese Enchiladas with Sweet Corn Salsa

Goat cheese is high in acid, so it calls for a fairly acidic red wine like an Anjou cabernet franc from France's Loire Valley or an Italian Chianti.

➤ Pan-Grilled Quesadillas with Chayote Slaw

The heat of hot pepper sauce and the richness of jack cheese make a really full-bodied white wine a good match. A semillon from Washington state, a white Rioja from Spain, or a greco di tufo from Italy would work. But let's admit it up front: If you empty half the bottle of pepper sauce into this, you'd better turn to ice-cold beer. Make it a Lone Star. Make it a case.

FOODS OF THE FAR EAST

➤ Black Pepper "Tenderloin" with Sesame Noodles

The peppery flavor of this dish brings two red wines to the fore: Merlot and Rhône wines based on the syrah grape can have both a peppery quality and the body to stand up to this strong flavor.

➤ Vegetable Curry with Toasted Rice Pilaf

Sweetness and spice: It's the kind of dish perfectly matched by white gewürztraminer. Again, both the slightly sweeter California style and the fuller-bodied, dryer, bolder variety from France's Alsace region are good choices.

CAJUN AND CARIBBEAN CUISINE

➤ Arroz con Garbanzo (Spanish Rice and Beans) with Tossed Greens

This dish is made with dry white sherry wine, and that is a perfect accompaniment to it. Either the fino or manzanilla style is nice. Careful, though—they're 14 percent alcohol, compared to 12 percent for most table wines.

➤ Bajan Macaroni Pie with Island Beet and Carrot Salad

The sweetness of ricotta and the sharpness of Cheddar call for a full-bodied red wine like cabernet sauvignon. But a tannic California cab is a bit too much. Try one from Chile or Australia. Or, surprise your guests with a soft and fruity cab from Mexico. No kidding.

INDEX

TABLE OF EQUIVALENTS

The exact equivalents
in the following tables
have been rounded
for convenience.

US/UK

oz=ounce

lb=pound

in=inch

ft=foot

tbl=tablespoon

fl oz=fluid ounce

qt=quart

METRIC

g=gram

kg=kilogram

mm=millimeter

cm=centimeter

ml=milliliter

l=liter

WEIGHTS

US/UK	METRIC
1 oz	30 g
2 oz	60 g
3 oz	90 g
4 oz (¼ lb)	125 g
5 oz (⅓ lb)	155 g
6 oz	185 g
7 oz	220 g
8 oz (½ lb)	250 g
10 oz	315 g
12 oz (¾ lb)	375 g
14 oz	440 g
16 oz (1 lb)	500 g
1 ½ lb	750 g
2 lb	1 kg
3 lb	1.5 kg

LENGTH MEASURES

⅛ in	3 mm
¼ in	6 mm
½ in	12 mm
1 in	2.5 cm

OVEN TEMPERATURES

FAHRENHEIT	CELSIUS	GAS
250	120	½
275	140	1
300	150	2
325	160	3
350	180	4
375	190	5
400	200	6
425	220	7
450	230	8
475	240	9
500	260	10

LIQUIDS

US	METRIC	UK
2 tbl	30 ml	1 fl oz
¼ cup	60 ml	2 fl oz
⅓ cup	80 ml	3 fl oz
½ cup	125 ml	4 fl oz
⅔ cup	160 ml	5 fl oz
¾ cup	180 ml	6 fl oz
1 cup	250 ml	8 fl oz
1½ cups	375 ml	12 fl oz
2 cups	1 l	32 fl oz